Unicycling

In this book, we have roughly rated the difficulty of the tricks and skills in order to show you if you have to expect more or less difficulties when you try to learn it.

Next to the chapter headings you will find one to three icons to show you the skill level.

 = Skill level 1

 = Skill level 2

  **= Skill level 3**

"The more icons are next to the chapter headings the higher the difficulty."

Unicycling
First Steps – First Tricks

Andreas Anders-Wilkens & Robert Mager

Meyer & Meyer Sport

Original title: Einrad fahren – Basics und erste Tricks
© 2006 by Meyer & Meyer Verlag, Germany
Translated by Andreas Anders-Wilkens
and Dr. Mark Berninger

British Library Cataloguing in Publication Data
A catalogue record for this book is available from the British Library

Unicycling – First Steps, First Tricks
Maidenhead: Meyer & Meyer Sport (UK) Ltd., 2007
ISBN: 978-1-84126-334-2

© 2007 by Meyer & Meyer Sport (UK) Ltd.
2nd Edition 2011
Auckland, Beirut, Budapest, Cairo, Cape Town, Dubai, Indianapolis,
Kindberg, Maidenhead, Sydney, Olten, Singapore, Tehran, Toronto
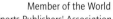 Member of the World
Sports Publishers' Association (WSPA)
www.w-s-p-a.org
Printed by: B.O.S.S Druck und Medien GmbH, Germany
ISBN: 978-1-84126-334-2
E-Mail: info@m-m-sports.com
www.m-m-sports.com

CONTENTS

Preface

Learning to ride a unicycle usually starts with a lot of unwanted detours. This was also true in our case. Unicycles were not very common when we started riding them in the early eighties. With some difficulty, you could buy one from a special manufacturer, but the idea of unicycling just for fun had not yet caught on. No written instructions for unicycling were available, and only a very few professional artists on unicycling were around to show others how it worked. So, we had to teach ourselves. Working alone and in small groups, we made some slow progress using the time-honored and time-consuming method of trial and error.

Today, getting a hold of a unicycle is a fairly easy matter. Specialty shops have sprung up in all major cities, and people can be seen riding unicycles almost everywhere in the streets. At least one unicycle can be found in even the smallest town. There are also more possibilities to learn from experienced riders. Our struggles have made us aware how important it is to pass on experience and special techniques that help one to avoid mistakes. This has taken us from just riding to actually teaching, and today we instruct people in the art of unicycling and other circus skills at our circus school "Zirkusschule Windspiel" which was founded in 2003. Among the children and teenagers we teach there, unicycling is by far the most favorite subject. Although girls in particular seem to be very fond of it, unicycling is by no means an all-female activity. The unicycling experience provides a unique mixture of athletic achievement, art, and enormous fun for everyone.

Despite the fact that unicycling has become a popular sport, there is still a need for written instruction since not everyone has a competent teacher within reach. We know from our experience with other circus skills (e.g. juggling) how helpful a small manual can be, and we have often lamented the lack of one on unicycling. The solution was to write one ourselves, which would help beginners from the start, and also contain some information for more experienced unicyclists, e.g. on new trends and developments.

The unicycle has, for example, moved out of the great towns where parks and squares have always offered good playgrounds. In the countryside, the versatile unicycle is now used for daring mountain unicycling (MUni) and for traveling long distances. The Internet offers a huge forum for unicycling, and all the spin-off activities associated with the sport. There is also more and more attention being paid to the athletic aspect of unicycling. In fact, this development seems to attract many young people, in particular. They want to show what they can achieve with a mixture of focused practice, and the fun of playing extraordinary games. World Championships with races, freestyle competitions, and hockey matches on unicycles are now being held biennially. In 2006 and 2008 the World Championships (called UNICON XIII and UNICON XIV) were held in Europe again after the last three took place in Tokyo, Bejing, and Seattle, Washington in 2004, 2002, and 2000 respectively. Unicycling has come home, so to speak, to Europe, where it has a long tradition of almost 150 years, and dates back to the time when bikes and unicycles were invented almost simultaneously.

Apart from the unicycle, no special equipment is needed to join the fun. You can get an affordable unicycle from any of the manufacturers listed at the end of the book. Here you will also find important tips on finding and buying the perfect, tailor-made unicycle for you. Proper shoes that cover your ankles are the only protection you need to wear at the beginning. If you are careful, and you do not mind an occasional minor bruise, you can even do without protective shoes. Later on, when you start doing some of the more daring moves on the unicycle, you can use the protective equipment designed for skateboarders.
We hope that you find this book helpful and you keep on unicycling, taking yourself to ever new experiences on one wheel.

To boldly go where no one has gone before.

A Learning to Ride a Unicycle
From Basics to Proficient Riding

1 How to Ride Forward

a) The Training Ground

When you start to ride a unicycle, your mind will be occupied with things other than **where you are going**. Since you will only be able to ride very short distances in the beginning, you don't really have to bother with much else. Artful dodging of obstacles and precise turns will have to wait until later.

So, in order to get started properly, you should find a place open enough. A few meters of clear ground all around you are necessary since you might find yourself going in directions you did not intend to go in.

Make sure that the place where you choose to practice is safe (no traffic!), and also that you don't endanger anyone else by what you are doing.

Please remember that it is prohibited to ride a unicycle on public roads since you could obstruct the traffic.

The ground you practice on should be firm and not slippery. An uneven piece of road might look like a bad training ground, but often it does not cause much of a problem because the unicycle is much less affected by it than you might think.

Really bumpy roads, grass, and gravel, on the other hand, are not really suitable. In addition, a slight downward slope is also less problematic than one that falls away to the side.

You can find everything you should know about your unicycle (adjusting the saddle, where the front/back is, etc.,) before you start riding it at the beginning of chapter **F 1**.

You don't really need a helmet or other protection as a beginner. You can't fall from great heights, and you can easily get your feet back on the ground. Protective clothing might even hinder your moving about freely. Only if you tend to injure easily should you take it upon yourself to wear some extra protection.

Before you start riding, you should **try to find something to hold onto**. People who can lend you a hand are ideal if they are available. Only hang on to your friends or parents as long as you need to in order to get used to your unicycle, and to learn how it reacts to you mounting, and to your movements.

In the following chapter, we will explain **how your assistants can best help you** on the unicycle. You will also learn how to practice properly with the help of only one or even no assistant at all using walls, fences, and other means of support. Don't start mounting your unicycle before you have found a suitable training ground, and some good assistants or support.

b)   Support and Assistants

If there is nobody around to help you, try to find something to hold onto like a fence, a handrail, or a wall. There shouldn't be any sharp edges or nails on top or along the wall.

Keep your hand open, and when you support yourself, avoid clinging to the fence or handrail. If your hands and arms cling too tightly, you will not learn to keep your balance properly. Stay in touching distance with the wall or fence without gripping it.

If the thing you hold on to is only available on one side, you will automatically tend slightly towards that side because you can only catch yourself from falling into the wall, but not away from it. Tending continuously to one side is of course bad for proper balance.

Much of the equipment usually found in a gymnasium (e.g. handlebars etc.) is extremely helpful. These are a great help to learn unicycling because you can arrange them, so that you get support from both sides. You can also place chairs or tables in a row to cycle along.

Having support at both sides is perfect to keep your balance. If gymnastic training boxes or bleachers are available, build them up as high as your shoulders.

However, chairs or special equipment are not always available. So, another good possibility is to use places like aisles, or narrow corridors, e.g. in your cellar or attic, where two parallel walls are often close enough to each other that you can touch both of them at the same time.

If it is not possible to find a place where you can hold onto both sides at the same time, one side will have to do. You should then **change direction** as often as possible, so you can learn to keep balance with a wall on your left side just as well as with a wall on your right side. Make sure that you keep some distance from the wall. Your arm's length is the right distance to avoid touching the wall with your pedal. This will also improve your balance since you avoid clinging to the wall.

A **shopping cart** is a great help. Hold the handlebars, and push the shopping cart when you practice. After closing, the often roomy parking lot of a shopping center is an ideal place to practice unicycling when no cars are around.

Support on one side offers some important help, and is better than no support at all.

The handlebars of a shopping cart provide support that moves along. Some garbage bins with wheels will do just as well.

A **short stick** held by someone is also a good means of assistance to you. If you are on the unicycle, you should hold onto the stick in front of you with both hands like the handlebars of a bike. The assistant should walk backwards holding the stick with both hands, as well. Make sure that you do not hurt your assistant with your falling unicycle when you dismount.

A **pole of about 2 meters** held by an assistant in the middle allows support for two or more children at a time. They can practice to ride in a circle, or perform in a show long before they can actually ride without help.

An old mast from a surfboard provides assistance for several children at a time.

Summary: Make sure you have good support. It should look like this:

- You should be supported **on both sides**, so that you can learn **to keep your balance on both sides.**
- A support on one side only **should be quite long** in order to allow you to ride for some time alongside the support before you have to turn around. Then, you can concentrate on the actual riding itself, rather than on turning around all the time.
- The support must be **solid and strong** because the unicycle tends to leave some marks and dents.
- It should be at least **as high as your hips,** and lower than your shoulders when you are on the unicycle, so that you can always keep your body straight.

The best and most flexible support is, of course, one or two assistants who can walk alongside offering help on demand. This can be done by other unicyclists if you share a unicycle with them, and use it alternately. It can also be your parents or some strong friends.

Important:

The assistants have to make sure that they do not disturb the balance of the unicyclist. They have to stay alongside the unicyclist the whole time to avoid pushing or pulling you without noticing it.

They should only offer support – like a walking post – and avoid actively holding the rider or the unicycle.

"You are not held by your assistant(s). They only offer support, and you should let go after a while. At first, you let go for a short while, and then for longer intervals whenever you feel balanced enough. Your assistant(s) stay at your side."

"This is the wrong way of helping. The assistant is lagging behind, and unbalances the unicyclist. The assistant should not raise his arm too high."

There is a general rule for any support that you might use while practicing:

Make sure that your goal is always to learn how to do it **without** support. Hold onto it just enough to avoid falling off the unicycle – not more and not less.

Very often, you will be tempted to not correct mistakes or, even worse, to learn movements the wrong way because the support or assistant is too readily available. If you keep in mind what it would be like without his or her support, you can actually **learn** something. Any support should mainly offer you a **safe feeling** on the unicycle until you become independent of the support.

Make sure that you don't hurt your assistant by holding too tightly on to his arms; he is your helpful assistant, not your victim.

c) Getting Started after All: Mounting Your Unicycle

After having chosen a suitable training ground and secured some good support or assistants, you can now actually start to learn unicycling. Your assistants could, of course, lift you up onto the saddle, or you could pull your body onto the saddle using your support; however, it is better to try to mount the unicycle on your own from the beginning. This way you will learn right away what is important.

Your assistants stand ready, but they don't offer help before you need it. If you have support on one side only, you should be within reach, but don't touch it right now. You have to do the first step on your own.

"You are ready for take-off. Try doing this on your own."

Put the unicycle in front of you with the narrow part of the saddle pointing forwards. Make sure that the position of the pedals is correct before you start mounting: The pedals should be almost at the same level with the one closer to you only a little lower than the other one.

Depending on which foot you would like to start with, the right or the left pedal should point towards you now. Hold the unicycle with your hands on both sides of the saddle.

"One pedal should be closer to you. This is where you put your foot first."

Move slowly towards the unicycle, and move your hands to the front of the saddle at the same time. Then, put the leg you want to start with over the saddle. Your whole weight is now on the other leg.

Now you put the saddle between your legs without changing the position of the pedals, and without moving the unicycle backwards or forwards. Then you put your foot on the pedal **without placing much weight on it right now.**

"Stand on one foot while you step over the saddle, and place the other foot on the pedal. Hold the saddle with both hands."

Keep one hand at the front of the saddle while reaching out with the other for **your assistant or your support at your side.**
Now, very, very slowly you can shift your weight from the foot you are standing on to the unicycle. Put **exactly as much weight on the saddle as on the one pedal.** Make sure that you keep your balance at all times. Your assistant or your support should not carry any weight; they are just there to help you to keep your **balance.** Repeat this movement up and down the pedal a few times until you feel you can do it almost without support.

"Your assistant or your support help to keep you balanced, but they do not carry your weight."
While you mount the unicycle, you can lean forward **a bit.** If you have done everything correctly, then your unicycle doesn't move away from you. It may move a bit towards you, though. In this way, it will move **slowly** under your body, and you can shift the remaining weight from the foot on the ground to the unicycle step by step.

Above: "Mounting slowly prevents injuries. A fast-moving pedal could hit your leg when you move too abruptly."
Left: "The initial position of the pedals does not change. The weight on the saddle is in balance with the force on the back pedal."

As soon as you have your whole weight on the unicycle, you can put the second foot on the other pedal. If you do everything slowly and with control, then the second pedal will **not** hit your shin.

If you step too fast onto the pedal, the unicycle will move, not only under your body but – if the pedal doesn't hit your leg – move beyond that point, and thus will get completely out of control.

At first it is better that all movements are done slowly, so you learn to coordinate them. Later, when you have become an expert, mounting a unicycle will be done in one smooth and quick movement.

"Mounting while using support on one side: Find your balance in the end with only ONE hand against the wall."

"Moving too abruptly, and putting too much weight on the pedal will make the unicycle move behind you."

Always keep in mind: beginners make large moves; experts make only small moves.

Mounting with the help of a wall, but without an assistant (see photos below):

- Push the saddle under your bottom. The pedals are in the right position.
- Put the first foot on the pedal closer to you. It is a bit lower.
- Move your weight forwards, and prop yourself up against the wall.
- Move the weight even more to the front, above the cycle and put the other foot on the second pedal.
- Move the pedals into a horizontal position. To do this, you might need to hold onto the wall, even with two hands if necessary. Make sure your feet are in the right position on the pedals.
- Straighten your body. Your center of gravity should now be exactly above the axis of your unicycle.

Mounting your unicycle **without** any help is much more difficult, but you don't have to learn it right now. Surely at this moment, you would rather learn how to ride. Mounting without help is explained below in *g) Free Mount.*

If you almost got it, but not quite: "I can't start properly!"

If, after mounting, your pedals got into the wrong position (one on top and the other one down), you can not start riding properly because both pedals are now in a deadlock position. This is the main advantage of controlling your power when you mount: your feet end up in the perfect position to **start** riding. So, you should make sure that your feet stay in the almost **horizontal** position you started with.

For a while, you might need to balance quickly with the help of some support, but soon you will be able to do it without any help.

"The left picture shows both pedals in a deadlock. You can hardly move from this position. The right picture shows the ideal position to cycle away."

Now take your time to concentrate, and finally prepare yourself for the start:

- Sit properly and upright. Your center of gravity should be in one line with the hub, saddle and head. The fork should be almost vertical
- Make sure your position on the pedals is ok. Correct this if necessary. If your feet are too close to the crank, you will scratch your ankle with the next turn, and become unbalanced. In addition, the balls of your feet should be on the pedals, not your toes!

"This is the right position on the pedal. Take care: being too close to the crank will scratch your ankle with the next turn."

Notice:

Mounting the unicycle is easier if the saddle is 2-3 cm lower than recommended in Chapter **F1. However**, don't forget to adjust it to the right position after you have practiced mounting.

d)   Free Riding

Stretch out both hands to keep your balance.
    Keep your body tense, and make sure that you stay upright. **Don't bend over.**

While riding, keep your body upright, and tilt forwards in order to get moving much like you do when you start walking.

"Keep your balance by stretching both arms to the side."
"Stay upright with some tension while you ride."

Only experienced or well-trained unicyclists, who can keep their body tense, can bend forward **a bit** to improve their balance.

In order to **move** forwards, you then pedal forwards.

The secret of successful unicycling lies in coordinating **these two movements:** The body is moving ahead, falling into the direction you would like to take. The feet move the unicycle forwards with the pedals to keep the unicycle under your body, and to prevent

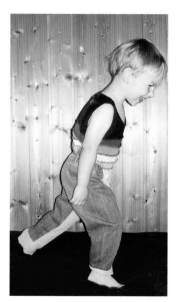

"When you start walking, you also have to tilt forwards first ..."
"... and then follow your weight with your feet."

"Beginners who are too cautious will step down from the unicycle backwards before they really get moving."

you from toppling. As long as you keep riding, the body's center of gravity is leading the unicycle a bit.

If you pedal too quickly, the unicycle gets in front of your body, and you inevitably fall backwards. This is a problem for those who are too cautious when they start riding.

On the other hand, those who are too eager to get going, tend to topple forwards.

"The reckless also tend to lose their balance and fall forwards."

If you hold the saddle of the unicycle behind you with one hand, you can keep it from falling on your heels, and hurting you when you have to step down. This is also a good way to protect your saddle from getting damaged. Don't try to hold the front of your saddle because your arm gets in your way while you are dismounting and trying to regain your balance running forwards.

A Final Instruction to Help You:

If you can't manage riding in a smooth forward pace, try (with additional support if needed) to do it like someone who learns to walk. Do it literally step by step. On a unicycle, this means that you move forward half-turn by half-turn. At first, your right foot is in front of you, then your left foot. For each half-turn, you move your front pedal carefully down, and when both pedals are in a horizontal position again, pause for a second and make sure that you still sit upright.

If this works well, then try it with a whole turn each time. At first the right foot is in front of you, and then you ride on until it is in front of you again. Stop! If this works well, try riding several turns at a time. The idea is to get those turns done in one smooth movement in order to blend these turns into a single, smooth movement. You will realize that you have suddenly managed to ride a few meters.

"You can learn step by step. Pause for a while when one foot has come to the front. Then, move the other foot."

Avoid false movements from the beginning. Don't perpetuate mistakes.

As soon as you have realized that you tend to repeat a certain mistake, you should stop and change your movements until the mistake and its effects are gone. If you had to jump from your unicycle three times in a row, you shouldn't repeat this mistake a fourth time. Otherwise, you will learn how to ride the wrong way, and it will become a habit, and it is very difficult to get rid of these wrong movements later.

Make sure that you keep riding with some speed once you have started, or you will have problems again with the pedals in what Charlie Dancey calls the "top dead center-position" in his book *How to Ride Your Unicycle*.

Once you have started, try to get into a smooth, steady forward movement. The slower you cycle, the more you will be busy keeping your balance because the "cyclist-unicycle" unit gets more stable with increasing speed - as long as you do not ride too fast and lose control. This time, it is really like riding a bike:
If you ride too slowly, you will lose your balance and fall over.
Make sure that you focus on something in the distance: If you look at the ground at the end of the gymnasium, for example, it will help you a lot to keep your balance. In this way, you will realize as early as possible if you are falling to one side. Then, you can correct your movements soon enough.

Summary:

You should keep the following in mind when you ride freely:

- Keep your body upright! Your spine should be in an almost vertical line with the saddle, and the hub of your unicycle.
- Look ahead at the ground at least 3 meters away from you, or better, focus on a point at the end of the room.
- Keep your legs, hips and back tense enough to control the unicycle.
- Put most of your weight on the pedals.
- Put about one third of your weight on the saddle.
- Keep your hands away from the saddle once you have mounted. Stretch your arms out instead in order to keep your balance.
- Ride with some speed, and don't be too cautious.
- Change direction from time to time if you have support on only one side.

e) Controlling Your Speed

You have just learned how unicycling, in principle, is done: You tilt in the direction you would like to take, and your feet continually pedal the unicycle forward to prevent you and the unicycle from actually toppling. This means you are sort of constantly falling on a unicycle. In order to gain speed, just **lean over** with your unicycle a bit more, but make sure that you keep your body straight all the time. Your head, the saddle, and the hub of your unicycle should still be aligned (see second photo below).

In order to go really fast, you may bend over a bit, and lean forward with the upper part of your body.

a: "Slow riding sitting upright."
b: "Riding fast by leaning forward to gain speed."
c: "This is a picture of an advanced unicyclist riding fast with the proper body tension. The bent-over position also enables you to stop abruptly."

Gaining speed must be done carefully because leaning forward just a few degrees may result in a drastic increase in the frequency of pedaling in order to keep the unicycle under your center of gravity.

By the way, stopping is done just the other way around: you reduce your speed by leaning backwards with your unicycle. This means that you need to pedal more slowly. Even riding backwards is done this way **(see A4).** It just takes some practice.

f)   Turns: Driving into the Direction You Want

It is almost more difficult to explain how to learn to take corners on a unicycle than it is to actually do it.

It is best compared to riding a bike: You do turns on the unicycle just the way you do it on a bike if you ride it **without your hands on the handlebars.** Certainly you have done or seen this before. Pay attention to the way a person's posture changes on the bike when somebody does this.

On the unicycle, lean toward the side you would like to turn into like you would do with a bike. At the same time, the upper part of your body should be tense and upright. You know this tense posture already. It enables you to keep your balance, and control your unicycle as much as possible, and this is true for turning corners, as well.

"Make your unicycle tilt with the help of your hips, but keep your body upright. A movement with your arms helps to start turning, and will make the turn more pronounced."

Next you should increase your speed a bit, and push down your inside pedal a bit. This is quite important – otherwise you will fall down to the side where you wanted to go, just like on a bike. You have to find out for yourself how heavily you have to lean to the side (often this becomes clear after you have tried it two or three times) and how much faster you have to go.

Finally, how you pedal, and what you do with the upper part of your body is important: press your thigh against the saddle into the direction you want to go. By turning your head, and the upper part of your body around (and by looking) into the direction you want to go shortly before you actually turn corners, you gain more control, and you also will see better where you are going. The way you pedal changes a bit, as well during a turn because the outside foot pushes to the inside at each turn of the crank when the pedal is in the top position. Use your arms to keep your balance while the upper part of your body turns to one side.

"Push the seat with your thigh into the direction you want to go."

You have to find out for yourself how to smoothly combine all these movements. While learning, you have practiced to ride in a straight line, and without knowing, you have already been making little turns all the time because it is impossible to really ride straight on a unicycle. It is constantly swerving to one side, and it never remains stable. Therefore, any movement in one direction is in fact a series of little turns to keep the line. By learning to accept these natural movements of a unicycle, and by simply emphasizing them a bit, if necessary, you will soon learn to go where you want to go without too much effort.

Here is a tip on how to make especially sharp turns:

> In order to turn abruptly, you have to stand up a bit, turn the upper part of your body in the direction you want to go, and turn the unicycle around completely using only your legs and feet, gaining momentum from your hips when the pedals are in a level position. Your arms support this movement.

g)   Free Mount

There are two variations of the free mount. Try both and find out which one suits you better. Make a clear decision which one you would like to practice before you start trying it. This will help you to avoid mixing up different movements from both variants.

We call these two variants **balance mount** and **idling mount.** The balance mount is smoother and more elegant, and you will need it for group freestyle, or if the space is limited. It also comes in handy if you have to start on a downward slope, or on ground where it is difficult to keep your balance. In order to learn the balance mount you have to overcome some difficulties at the beginning. But, on the other hand, you already tackled these difficulties when you learned this mount **with** support.

The idling mount is easier at first, but it requires more courage. You need it, for example, to start uphill.

For the **balance mount,** put the pedals in the position shown on page 32. The lower pedal is next to you. Then, you push the saddle between your legs back to your bottom without changing the position of the pedals. Now it is time to take your hand away from the saddle in order to better keep your balance with it. In a smooth and well-controlled movement, you shift your whole weight onto the unicycle now, still without changing the position of the pedals. Your head and your upper body move forward in a smooth movement, and you start riding the unicycle straight away. So, your feet stay for a moment in a balancing position before they actually start pedaling.

Mounting with support (see chapter 1c) has already shown you in practice which forces have to be kept in balance: by putting more weight on the pedal closer to you, the unicycle gets an **impulse** to move backwards, but you can avoid this backward movement by balancing this with the forward momentum gained by your body.

The forward momentum is transferred to the unicycle by putting part of your weight on the saddle. The leg that is still on the ground pushes you forward now, while in movement, you shift the rest of your weight forwards, and onto the unicycle. By pushing your hips against the saddle between your legs, you push the unicycle forwards.

If both forces are kept in complete balance, the unicycle will stay perfectly still. Even the pedals will stay in their position, and a well-controlled mount becomes quite easy.

Take your second foot from the ground, put it on the second pedal, and start pedaling with this foot as soon as your center of gravity has moved forward and passed the axis. Take your second foot from the ground and put it on the front pedal. Leave only one hand on the saddle to use the other to steady yourself while you are moving your whole weight onto the unicycle without changing the position of the pedals. This should be done in one smooth and well-controlled movement with your head and upper body leaning forward. Your feet should keep still for a moment while you find the balance. Then you can start pedaling with the front foot first as your center of gravity has moved forward and past the axis of the unicycle.

"In a balance mount, your unicycle does not move backwards before you start riding."

For the **idling mount,** put the pedal into the position shown in the first picture on the next page. Push the saddle between your legs as usual, and put your foot on the pedal next to you, but don't put any weight on it yet. Then, you move forwards while you carefully co-ordinate the following movements. Put more and more weight on the pedal, and gradually lift your second foot. Make sure that you lift your toes a bit, as well to get the whole foot on the pedal.

Shifting your weight slowly onto the first pedal will prevent the second pedal from hitting your shin.

The upper part of your body and your shoulders remain in position while the unicycle moves backwards for about a third of a turn.

For the idling mount, it is important that the forces are **not** in balance. The force that moves your unicycle backwards by stepping onto the pedal next to you is stronger. This way the unicycle is forced to move backwards right under your body. The pedal you stepped on first is moved **forwards** at the same time to the front of the unicycle, and from this position it is then possible to simply start pedaling forwards as soon as your unicycle has moved a bit behind your body.

"Make sure to shift your balance correctly when you do the idling mount. The unicycle moves backwards when you shift your weight from the ground to the seat and pedals."

Tips for Both Variants

In both cases, as soon as your second foot is on the pedal, you must wait a fraction of a second before you can actually start riding because if you do not wait, your body will lag behind, and the unicycle will tip from under you and you will fall backwards. This moment of complete balance is needed in both variants, and it is the reason why the free mount is so difficult for the beginner. Only if you have managed to end up balanced after mounting the unicycle, will you be able to stay on it long enough to actually start riding.

Keep in mind that control over the pedal when you put your foot on it does not only depend on how much weight you put on the pedal, but also on how quickly you move. Try to find the right mixture for yourself by repeating the complicated first steps of the mount over and over again without actually starting to ride until you end up balanced on the unicycle.

 # 2 First Obstacles

You will have to master riding over small obstacles from a very early stage.

You will probably ride your unicycle not only in a gymnasium or a similar place where the conditions are very good, but you will soon find yourself spending a lot of time on bumpy ground like backyards, playgrounds, country trails, parking lots, lawns and so on. If you do not want to dismount your unicycle at every curb, or have to drive around every little rock, you better become skilled at riding on unleveled ground. Take it as a challenge! You can already start this training in the gym by riding over ropes, hockey-sticks or any other smaller objects available.

Descending from small steps, or riding on a grassy lawn isn't much of a problem really. Don't think about it too much; just try it.

Riding uphill, climbing steps or keeping on a narrow path is more challenging, so is riding on metal grates, or on extremely bumpy or soft, wet, and slippery ground. But, with some practice you will soon master conditions you thought almost impossible before. The unicycle is very versatile, and it is great fun to explore all its possibilities.

a)   Steps

It is quite easy to ride off a curb.

The only thing you have to be careful about is the speed you will suddenly gain when you descend. Therefore, when you reach the edge, you should lean back a bit. (Remember? This is what we told you not to do when you started riding!) This way you can **slow down** as soon as you have descended, and get into an upright position again.

"Make sure that you slow down and use your body as a shock absorber when you descend. It is best to land with your pedals level in order to distribute weight onto both feet. Do also lean forward a bit, and rise somewhat from the seat."

It is a good idea for a beginner to ride along the edge of the curb until the pedals are in the right position to ride off. Low steps are best taken with level pedals, while you should descend from high steps with the pedal in a vertical position. This means that you can immediately start to slow down as soon as you have landed. Make sure to turn **sharply** at the edge, and ride down the edge at a right angle to the curb as soon as your pedals have reached the correct position in order to avoid scraping the edge with one pedal which might unbalance you.

If you descend 10 cm or more, you must put much weight on your pedals first, and ride your unicycle while you are standing **(see chapter 5.)**. This will take most of the impact of the descent. Keep the seat in place by holding it with both thighs, and one hand if necessary.

"Without looking, you should start to learn which position your pedals are in. Then, you will develop a feeling when it is right to tackle the obstacle."

When you want to climb a step, the position of the pedals is important, as well. Make sure that you meet the edge at a right angle with considerable speed. Step heavily on the front pedal in order to climb the step. This is actually quite similar to the normal movement you make when you climb a step without a unicycle. Your stronger leg should be in front then. Shortly before you hit the edge, lean backwards and bend over a bit because you will be thrown forward when your unicycle is stopped by the step.

"If you descend more than 10 cm, you should take your weight off the seat, and put it on the pedals where you can absorb the impact of the descent with your knees. Hold the seat with one hand while the other helps you stay balanced."

"When you hop sideways, you should ideally stand still first, and then lean sideways sufficiently before you hop. Overcome the reflex to immediately hop back."

Make sure that your tire has enough air-pressure when you do any of these tricks because you might damage your unicycle otherwise!

Of course, you can also try to hop up and down steps, or jump over smaller obstacles once you have learned that trick (see chapter B10). In order to do so, you slowly move diagonally towards the edge. Stand up somewhat just before you jump, and lean sideways into the direction you want to jump. Practice this first on a fairly flat step.

"Lean back and bend over a bit to balance the jolt when you come down. Also, rise somewhat out of the seat."

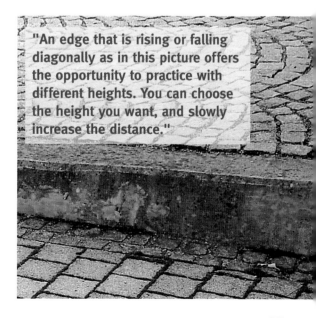

"An edge that is rising or falling diagonally as in this picture offers the opportunity to practice with different heights. You can choose the height you want, and slowly increase the distance."

b) Narrow Paths

Riding along narrow paths, and on wooden planks or even wooden beams is a great challenge because this allows you to **pick and choose a specific level of difficulty for yourself.**

Start practicing on paved ground. Draw two parallel lines on the street surface with chalk. They should be 30 cm apart and about 10m long. Try staying between the lines on your unicycle. Once you have mastered the 30 cm without riding across one of the lines, you can make the distance narrower, and see if you can still keep within the lines. You can also practice to ride on a line. The chalk lines allow you to cheat here and there while you are not entirely proficient. It doesn't matter if you ride across a line occasionally as long as you keep practicing.

"Riding along wooden beams, on small walls, or even across trees which lie on the ground looks spectacular, feels great, and isn't that difficult."

It is a special challenge to ride along wooden planks without help. This needs a combination of different moves. First, step up with the unicycle to get on the plank, then keep on it, and finally, get off it again. Cheating is impossible now.

The narrower your plank is the more difficult it gets, of course. With really narrow planks, you have to be careful because they tend to tip and to topple if you get too close to the edge.

Riding on the benches that are usually found in a gymnasium proves to be great fun. At first, you get somebody to help you, and you can put mats on both sides, so that you feel safer. You ride along without any help. Advanced unicyclists can build a **square of four benches,** and practice turning corners on benches, as well. You can even build a ramp to get on and off the benches with the unicycle. Three wooden springboards make a good ramp if they are available. You can even try riding off the benches without a ramp, but this takes some practice. Make sure that your weight is on the pedals, and the ball of each foot is properly on the pedals, as well.

Get somebody to assist you when you ride off a bench the first time. Your assistant(s) should make sure that you do not fall to the side or backwards, but they shouldn't actually lift you down.

"To assist the unicyclist in riding down high steps, the helper should support him with an underarm grip, and aid in keeping the balance by holding the rider's elbow."

Just before you reach the end of the bench, start riding standing up in order to avoid hurting your crotch when you come down from the bench. Ride towards the edge slowly. Hold the seat with one hand, and pull the whole unicycle up somewhat which will increase the contact of your feet with the pedals, and help you keep control over the unicycle when you come down. Keep on riding to the end. Now ride across the edge, and make sure that both legs are extended and tense.

"Balancing high above ground feels safer with some help."

At the edge, your assistant supports you by holding your elbow with one hand, and supporting you with an underarm grip with the other hand. When you fall, part of your weight is carried by the underarm grip, and the hand at the elbow keeps you in balance. Your assistants should walk along, and stay next to your wheel at all times. This method of assisting someone on the unicycle can be used for other difficult and dangerous tricks, like riding down a stairwell, as well.

If you happen to lose your balance while riding on a bench, or if you can not stay on your chosen path anymore, it is often a good idea to turn a corner sharply to the side, and ride off the bench at a right angle while your unicycle is still under control. Sliding diagonally off the edge can be dangerous because your pedal might get caught on the edge in this way, and throw you in midair off the unicycle. If you realize that you are actually losing control, it is usually not too late for a controlled landing. Never just jump off your unicycle uncontrollably. As long as you stay in contact with the saddle and the pedals, you are in fact well protected. Wait until you know for sure to which side you are falling. Use this time to prepare to soften the crash. After some practice, you will be surprised how much you can still do while falling. Learning how to fall properly without a unicycle is taught in many martial arts like judo or aikido. It might be a good idea to do a crash course in falling techniques there.

Think safety first when you do advanced moves, and remember the following rule: **get off the unicycle while you can still choose, and not when you are forced to.**

You will become more self-assured by minimizing your mistakes right from the start, and not by taking the unnecessary risk of falling. (See also D1a)

c)   Bumpy Ground

A nice first exercise for riding on bumpy ground is riding up and down over some springboards arranged in a line in the gym.

Riding on gravel, on sand, in high grass or unpaved ground will then test your skill. Keep your body upright and tense while you put even more weight than usual on the pedals. Keep in contact with the pedals, and put your weight on the pedals consciously, rather than just riding forward. Stretch out your arms a bit. With one hand you can grip the seat loosely to keep it under control.

"Feel the bumps in the ground with your feet. Do not look at the ground, but straight ahead and keep upright."

"Prepare to bend down early enough while you ride towards the object you want to pick up"

 # 3 Picking Things Up from the Floor

For this trick, it is helpful to adjust the seat to a **low** position. Keep upright until you have almost reached the bottle (or whatever you try to pick up) and bend down to the side, slowly passing the point where it stands, and come up again. You can also start idling next to the bottle (see A.5) and pick it up when your pedals are almost level.

Don't be complacent: Pick up a 1.5 l bottle first, then take smaller ones, and finally you can even pick up an apple, or a bottle on its side. Picking up a coin from the ground is really a high-end trick, just like putting a bottle **back** where you had picked it up! By varying the amount of water in a bottle, the level of difficulty of this trick can be easily changed: Putting back an empty bottle is much more difficult than a half-filled one.

"Pay attention to the correct position of the pedals when you pick up objects."

B First Tricks
and Artistic Skills

1 Riding Backwards

It doesn't matter which you learn first: riding backwards or idling **(see B.2).** As soon as you have mastered the one, it is quite easy to learn the other as well because idling is nothing more than riding a short distance backwards and forwards over and over again to remain more or less in the same spot!

Just as when you are riding forwards, you have to lean into the **direction you want to go,** so lean backwards to ride. In the beginning, this might take some courage. Make sure that there is enough space behind you and to the sides because you can not turn corners properly riding backwards yet.

You should look back over your shoulder as often as possible in order to see where you are going.

The balance mount (see A1g) is the natural choice when you want to get on the unicycle and ride backwards straight away. This way you can put your second foot on the pedal and start riding at once because your body is already leaning backwards.

"Practice looking back over your shoulder right from the very beginning."

Important:

Ride carefully and control your speed. If you have to dismount at a high rate of speed, you will not be able to slow the rate of speed down by running to a stop, and falling backwards onto the ground is practically inevitable. Prepare to do a backward roll if necessary to soften the fall.

"Look back over your shoulder before you start riding to make sure that nothing is in the way. Then, look ahead, mount, and start riding backwards."

All the equipment you have used to learn to ride forwards is of course now useful again.

Important:

If you learned how to idle first, then you can proceed like this: start idling, ride a short distance backwards with one or two turns of the wheel, and then start idling again. This way, you will also learn how to slow down and how to accelerate when moving.

 # 2 Idling

Idling means that you hover over a spot without dismounting.

The various ways, both basic and advanced, of how you can idle are presented below. Idling takes some time and some practice to learn, but you should definitely try it because it's well worth it.

Basic idling:

The best way to learn idling is to practice any place where you can hold onto something on both sides, e.g. between two doorposts. Make sure that the door has no threshold because you will need even ground.

Since you need just a small spot to practice, idling can be learned in all sorts of places. Support yourself on both sides, but only as much as you need. It is also possible to learn idling with support on only one side; however, it is more difficult.

If you have a 20-inch unicycle or smaller:

- start idling with the pedals in a level position
  (if your wheel is bigger than 20 inches, then the front pedal should be a bit higher)

- ride backwards almost a half turn and forwards again at once, without moving your head and shoulders,

- repeat this rocking back and forth motion in quick succession, and hold onto both sides,

- use the support only as much as necessary.

When you get the hang of it, you can reduce the distance you ride to **a quarter of a turn**. The movement gets easier this way because it takes less effort since now you don't have to move the weight of your body much.

"Imagine that your head and shoulders stay in the same position, and that only the wheel is pedaled back and forth. Every turn is initiated by your lower foot."

You can now also try the so-called freeze: don't move your wheel at all, keeping your balance just with the movement of your upper body.

Important tips:

Head and shoulders stay in the same position all the time! Only the wheel and the lower part of your body move back and forth. The pedal is moved forwards as far as it is moved backwards.

Most of the work is done with the lower foot. It takes the lead for the transition from moving forwards to backwards and to forwards again. Much of your weight – about half of it – rests on the lower foot, in particular at the two transition points. The other half of your weight remains on the saddle, of course. The upper foot just follows along. Make sure that your foot does not slip off the pedal on this side because this foot should be lightly touching the pedal.

The most difficult thing is keeping your balance on each side.
If you start to fall to one side, then try to turn the whole unicycle in that direction as soon as possible: This means that you transform your "falling to one side" into either "falling forwards," or into "falling backwards" if you can already turn the unicycle backwards. Your forward or backward balance can be kept quite easily while you are idling by riding forwards or backwards just a little bit faster. Practice turning to the left or to the right while idling in order to be able to balance yourself. Arms and shoulders guide a turn to the side.

"Your arms guide the turn to one side or the other."

3 Idling with One Leg

"Idling with only one leg is less difficult than it looks!"

Idling with one leg is easier than you might think. As you have learned already, idling with both feet is done mostly with the lower foot. This means that taking the upper foot off the pedal entirely is not a big deal.

First, practice taking the foot off for only a short time by stretching it forward to the front shortly before the upper pedal is about to change direction from forwards to backwards.

Your lower foot is already starting to work to change the momentum at that time. Put the upper foot on the pedal again as soon as the pedal actually starts to move backwards. You might have to "chase" the pedal a bit to get the foot back in place. Repeat taking the foot off and putting it back on until you can keep it off the pedal for a fairly long time. You will find that you can now idle without the second foot. The best place to rest your free foot is the shafts just above the wheel (see photo). Make sure that your foot doesn't touch the wheel!

"Try to find new positions for your free leg."

You can try to find other positions for your foot and your entire leg: stretched out in front, or to the side, or crossed over the other leg.

A funny trick is to pretend like you are trying to put the foot back on the pedal, but you keep missing it each time because the pedal is exactly at the opposite position.

"Help, where has my pedal gone?!"

"While mounting, begin with the left pedal in a level position with the right foot if your left foot is your favorite foot."

4 Idling on One Side or Crank Idling

This trick is quite impressive for any audience! The best way to learn it is to have a wall on the opposite side of your unicycle and to tackle a mounting without support after you have mastered the trick itself. Having a wall on the other side will prevent you from falling on your unicycle and getting hurt.

If you stand on the pedal, the saddle is pressed against your outer thigh. This means that you actually don't have to hold it, but you can do so in the beginning if you want.

"Make sure to dismount the saddle only towards the free side. You might get hurt if you try to get off on the other side because the inside foot is often stuck, and cannot move freely."

51

Unlike normal idling, **both** feet are active in this trick. The outer foot on the pedal should be your favorite foot. The inner foot on the crank (see photo) usually carries most of the weight. Only when the movement of the pedal has to change its direction, do you have to shift your weight from the inner foot to the one on the pedal. Other than in normal idling, you can't go back and forth so far that the pedals get in a horizontal position. You have to change direction half way when the pedal has moved about 45 degrees.

"Shifting your weight gives the impulse for each turn. Make sure that the pedal goes up much less than in normal idling."

A fancy finish is to lift your inner leg over the saddle and put it on the other pedal. Continue to idle the normal way now.

"If you are an expert in keeping your balance, try this."

5 Riding while Standing and Pulling the Seat Away from the Body

You have already learned how to take the seat away when you were practicing riding down steps **(see A 2a)**. What was then meant as protection against injury can also be turned into a technique which allows you to do a series of tricks.

One of them is taking the seat away. In order to do so, you stand up while you are riding or idling (see p. 54). It helps a lot to ride with bent knees.

If you fix the seat in a position lower than usual (about 3-5 cm) it gets much easier to pull it away from your body. Hold the seat at the side, and pull it out behind you. Your hand stays close to your inner thigh. Most people feel that riding with the saddle in back is easier, and pulling it out to the back is also easier because the front of the saddle is narrower.

"Stretch your legs out as much as possible while riding to get off the seat."

In order to show your audience that the seat is pulled free, you should hold it at the very front, and push it back as far as possible. Use your free hand to keep the balance.

"First, grip the seat at the side when you take it away. Then, move along the rim to hold it at the front."

"Taking the seat away backwards is easier than taking it away to the front. If you can hold it in mid-air behind you, your audience will be impressed."

Tip:

Tightly press the arm which is tightly holding the seat at the side of your body to your side. This will help to keep up the tension.

"Start riding while you hold the seat behind you."

Instead of pulling the seat away while you are riding, you can also **start** with the seat already behind you.

"When you have learned to ride with the seat pulled away you can bend at the knees, and hold the bar which supports the seat between your legs. Can you ride now without holding the seat with your hands?"

You can also pull the seat away to the front. Stand up, and take the front of the seat, and pull it away. As soon as your seat is free, pull **up** hard, and hold tightly in order to increase the contact of your **feet** with the pedals. It is also possible to take the seat away while you are idling. Just try it!

"Put the same weight on both feet even if your bent posture suggests otherwise, and stick the seat against the outside of your hip. Don't touch the wheel with your shin."

It is quite easy to take the seat away while you are idling and then stick it against your outer hip. Start practicing this with some support at your side.

6 Stomach on the Seat- Airplane Trick

"Start while holding onto something or take the seat away to the front while riding."

For this fairly easy but impressive trick, you first have to take the seat away to the front. This can be done before or after you have started riding. As soon as your seat is in front of you, place your stomach on the seat, but make sure that you don't stop pedaling. Put only as much weight on the seat as necessary to keep it under control. About half of your weight should remain on your pedals. Stretch out your arms to the side to make it look better.

"By keeping up the tension in your arms and body you will be able to put about half of your weight on the seat, and you will develop the knack of steering only with your legs."

We recommend that you fix the seat in a higher position for the "stomach on seat." On the other hand, then removing the seat from riding position gets more difficult. This shows that the height of your seat is important for certain moves, but it is often difficult to find an ideal position.

"Look, I'm a plane."

You can also try to put the seat back between your legs and sit upright again while you are still riding.

7 Preparation for Riding the Ultimate Wheel – Drag Seat

This trick is a good way to practice for the ultimate wheel **(see chapter C)**; in particular, if a proper ultimate wheel is not available.

You should do this trick on a smooth surface, e.g. in a gymnasium, in order to protect the seat. It also gets stuck on the ground easily otherwise.

A good way to learn drag seat is riding with the seat in back (or in front, see B5). Make sure that you only hold the seat lightly now.

Now, pull the seat away to the front while riding, and drop it to the floor from your outstretched hand in order to start the drag seat trick. Don't bend over when you drop the seat.

"Drop the seat from your outstretched hand. You can pick the seat up again while you are riding. Reach out for the seat without shifting your center of gravity forwards."

Keep on riding, making sure that you keep your balance by shifting your weight correctly back and forth between the pedals. If you are too slow in shifting the weight, you will fall to the side. Bending at the knees is a good idea. This also helps to get the seat as low as possible before you drop it. It will then bounce off the floor less, and you can keep your unicycle more easily under control.

If you have a big wheel, it may touch your calves a bit without disturbing you whereas a small wheel won't touch your legs at all. With a big wheel, the rubbing against your calves may even help to keep the wheel in balance. To protect your skin, you should wear sturdy baggy jeans.

You can drop the seat in front of you or behind you. The name "drag seat" indicates that the real trick is to drop it behind you, of course.

You will find that dragging the seat across the floor actually helps to keep the balance like the tail of a cat. Sudden changes in direction, however, are not possible though for the same reason. Make sure to pedal evenly, keeping your legs tense.

"A big wheel with little or no tread and baggy trousers might do the trick instead of many hours of practice."

"Your eyes don't lie:
The seat can be picked up with your heel from
behind while you are riding."

8 Spinning

Spinning means to push yourself away from some means of support (e.g. a wall) in order to spin around in one spot. Later, you can practice to spin without any help. At that point, it is similar to constantly turning corners.

Ride towards the wall, slow down, and get your **upper** body upright. Keep your upper body in this posture until the spin is over. Push against the wall with one hand, against the direction into which you are riding right now. Do this slowly, but with some force involving your shoulder and your hip to do at least a 180° spin. Spinning 360° isn't much more difficult because you can continue riding into the same direction afterwards. Make sure that you keep upright while spinning. For a 360° spin, you should look straight ahead into the direction you are riding as long as possible in order to stay orientated. Meanwhile your eyes should overtake the turning of the body, and find a focal point in the original direction again before your body has finished the spin. Wait until your whole body has finished the spin and ride on.

It is an impressive trick when two unicyclists meet riding from opposite directions, and their outstretched right hands push off of each other. This way both can spin, and then ride on.

"Use your shoulders and your hip to gain force when you push away slowly from the wall. Your arms are the last to follow the rest of your body and before the body has finished the spin, you already look ahead again."

"Idle forward as far as possible."

"When your pedal has reached the highest position in backward idling, lean forward, and start pedaling determinedly, but not hastily."

9 Riding with One Leg

The possible positions where you might place your free foot are described above in **"B3 Idling with one foot"**.

Idling with one foot is good preparation for riding with one foot. Start idling, and try to rock back and forth as far as possible in that you lean forward and backward as much as possible.

Now, the pedal that is at the highest point is almost level or even better, higher. Start riding now while pedaling energetically to make sure that you have enough power in order for the pedal to make more than a full turn. Your foot must remain in constant contact with the pedal even when it moves around the back towards its highest, vertical position. You will automatically slow down the pedal somewhat with your foot when it goes up at the back. Therefore, you have to pedal even harder when you start, but make sure that you keep control over your unicycle during this sudden movement. Lean forward quite a bit when you start in order to stay on the unicycle.

Be sure to pedal hard the **second** time once you have managed to make a full turn because you will still need much more speed. Only after 2-3 turns will you be fast enough to ride along smoothly.

If you want to stop, get slower bit by bit, and then stop **abruptly** by pushing hard on the pedal when it comes up again. You can switch to idling now or dismount.

Another possible way to learn riding with one foot is to start by lifting one foot off the pedal for a fraction of a second while riding. Each time the left pedal is at the top position, lift your left foot briefly, and put it back down again. Now, try to prolong the time it is off the pedal until you can ride entirely without it.

Riding with one foot only is somewhat dangerous as you have too ride quite fast to keep rolling. Therefore, please take extra care.

10 Hopping

A perfect way to learn hopping on a unicycle is to do it consciously first without a unicycle. Hop on the balls of both feet at the same time, and take the jump with straight knees and only pushing off from your ankles and arms.

Next, try hopping with your feet as if they were on the pedals of the unicycle, i.e. slightly apart and one foot in front of the other.

Begin your practice session while standing on the unicycle with one hand at the saddle and the other holding onto some means of support. The pedals are in a level position, and the balls of your feet are on the pedals. This will allow you to use the springing force from your ankles most efficiently. You need to learn to pull the unicycle up against your feet in order to maintain contact in the air with the pedals. Pull your unicycle up with one hand at the saddle while the other hand helps to keep your balance.

Keep your overall balance by hopping in the direction in which you begin to fall. This way, you can keep the axis of the unicycle exactly under your center of gravity. Once you have mastered this, you should try to learn hopping without a hand on the saddle.

By pointing your toes inwards towards the unicycle, your thighs turn a bit until you can touch the saddle with the muscles at the front of your thighs.

"It is not important how high you jump, but rather that you keep your body in an upright position."

"As you have learned in the practice session, you need to hop on the balls of your feet. If you lose contact with one of the pedals you will lose control over your unicycle and crash. To avoid this, pull your unicycle up against your feet with one hand."

Now, you can grip the saddle with your inner thigh muscles while standing. At the same time, your ankles must remain relaxed in order to be able to jump.

Remember: It's mainly the ankles that make you hop.

You can hop standing (see also A2) and even spin around while hopping. Use your hip in order to make 90° turns at first, and then after some practice, you can proceed to 180° spins or, hop forwards or to the side.

Important:

Make sure you keep contact with the pedals at all the times to avoid crashing and hurting yourself!

At first, holding the saddle with your thighs hurts a bit, and you will have to take a break quite frequently. Make sure you don't rub yourself raw on the inside of your thighs with the saddle. You can only avoid this by pressing your thighs really hard against the saddle by tensing the muscles, but not bending at the knees. Thus, your **skin** will not move up and down against the saddle. Instead, the resulting "massage" of your **muscles** is much less painful than the constant rubbing of the skin.
Wearing cycling shorts might help a bit, as well.

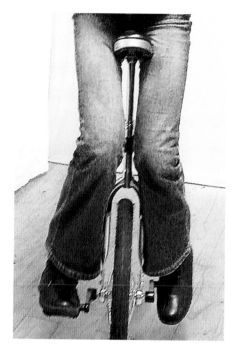

"Pull the saddle up with your thighs."

Important:

Keep upright, and don't bend at your knees. Instead, try to use your arms, shoulders, and your back to support your ankles in the hopping.

11 Rope Skipping on the Unicycle

Use a thin solid plastic jump rope with handles. You should first learn how to do rope skipping without the unicycle, but you don't have to be a rope skipping expert.

"A solid plastic rope moves fast through the air, and can be handled easily on the unicycle."

For rope skipping on the unicycle, your rope should be about 10cm longer than a normal rope. Hold both handles in one hand, and get on your unicycle. Next, start hopping. Pull the saddle up with your free hand if you want. Now, continue without the hand on the saddle, and get upright, hopping all the time.

"Hold both handles in one hand at the beginning."

Now, start swinging the rope at your side to work out good timing of hopping and jumping: each time your rope touches the floor your unicycle should be high up in the air. Keep up this rhythm now while grabbing one handle with your second hand. Take a handle in each hand, and separate them just before the rope is way above you, so that both hands are in the final position for jumping.

Important:

Finding the right timing, and keeping the rhythm of hopping and jumping is the most difficult thing. The best timing for a beginner is to hop twice while you only jump the rope once. This way, you don't have to jump too high and can do low, targeted hops instead.

This might (also) help you to find the right rhythm: During the first hop, **start** pulling the rope **apart while it is still behind you** as you are on your way up into the air. The rope has then just passed your head when you are back on the floor again, and when your hands are at your sides. When you do the **second** hop now, the rope comes around exactly in time to skip under your unicycle. This timing is useful because it also helps you a lot to keep your balance.

"Before you start swinging the rope, you should be hopping evenly and smoothly. The rope is held with two hands behind your back ready to start."

This 2:1 timing gives you the chance to move slowly, and keep full control. The hopping and skipping movements support each other when both, rope and unicycle, move **up and down** simultaneously with the first hop. With the second hop, your movements support each other when your unicycle moves up and skips the rope moving down. The unicycle should land shortly after the rope has passed under it because then it is **not** at the highest position in the air anymore. So, you should hop rather too early than too late. This helps to keep the balance as well.

Swing the rope just fast enough, and hop slowly enough in order to match **two** hops with one turn of the rope. Later, you can swing the rope much faster, and slow your hopping down a bit to do only one hop for each skip. It can also help to keep up exactly the same rhythm of hopping and swing the rope even faster to change from the 2:1 into the 1:1 rhythm.

"Pictured here, the position of the rope and the unicycle will allow the rope to skip just in time with the second hop in a 2:1 rhythm."

"With a 1:1 rhythm, rope and unicycle should be in this position, too: the rope has already passed above the head, and is in front of you when the unicycle is at the lowest position (as indicated by the flat tire!)."

Tip:

Make sure that the rope dangles freely behind you when you start jumping because it can easily get stuck at the back of your unicycle, or on the pedals.

If you have two people to help you, they can swing a long rope for you. They can even be on unicycles themselves, and you can then change places, as well. If they swing the rope (instead of you doing it) you can better concentrate on the hopping and riding. Maybe this is the start of a new routine for a public performance.

Start riding in an upright position between the two people swinging the rope **in front of you at a right angle.** This way, you can idle in front of the swinging rope, and find out the right moment to get into the middle. The rope should move towards you over the floor because then it moves away from you when you get close to it and into the center position.

Ride towards the two people swinging the rope at a right angle. Stop shortly before the swinging rope to find the right moment to get into the middle. Ride into the middle quickly trailing the rope, and you will have enough time to start hopping while it moves upward in front of you and over your head. However, it will now come down behind you so you must have a feel for the timing for the first jump. Turn around while hopping until you can see the rope coming down.

Stopping at the point where the rope almost touches you in mid-air before you ride into the middle might help you get used to the situation if you find that you are afraid of the rope. You can then wait until you are in tune with the rhythm, and you are ready to start.

You can also try the following: when you ride in directly after the rope has moved away from you across the floor, you have a lot of time to ride through the middle, and come out at the other side while the rope swings overhead.

Tip:

Try also getting to the center position coming from the one side where the rope ends. This can be better because you can get to the center position easier without touching the rope.

C Variations on the Unicycle

1 Giraffe

a) Preparing to Mount

A tall unicycle with a chain is called a "giraffe."

It is easy to ride a giraffe! It just takes some courage. The giraffe weighs considerably more than a normal unicycle and therefore it reacts somewhat more slowly to your movements. This can be advantageous, as well because it takes a longer time for it to fall, and you have more time to react if you get into trouble. You will need to move slowly and powerfully. After a short while, you will realize that the differences are not that great as you grow more accustomed to the new feelings on the ultimate. It is, however, important to buy the right giraffe that really suits you (see chapter F1).

"The giraffe is a tall unicycle with a chain."

In the beginning, you will need support to mount the giraffe. Try to find a table, wall, tree, or anything else which is between 80 and 120 cm high and strong enough to carry your weight easily. As always, find a place that is safe (no traffic!) for practice. Make sure that you don't endanger anyone else by what you are doing because a giraffe is quite heavy, and might injure someone. Tie your shoelaces tightly and put them firmly into your socks or shoes, if necessary, because a shoelace can easily get caught around your pedal or crank and obstruct pedaling. If this happens, you will inevitably fall down from the giraffe and hurt yourself.

If one or two people are around, you can ask them to hold the giraffe while you are mounting. For the first few rides on the giraffe, it is very good to have someone to hold your hand.

No matter how you mount a giraffe with or without support, there are some rules you should know and follow: Move slowly and don't jump, keep close to the pole of the giraffe and don't let the saddle go until you sit on it, pull yourself onto the giraffe by using the shoulder of your assistant.

Make sure that the pedals stay in a **vertical** position all the time, in particular when you hold onto the saddle a bit while mounting.

The assistants block the wheel with one foot in front and another one behind it for the whole time while you are mounting. This blocking is the most important help for your mounting. If there is only one assistant, then both of his feet should block the wheel as shown in the picture. The upper pedal should point towards the assistant. His hands hold the pole of the giraffe just below the saddle.

"Both feet of the assistant block the wheel. The hands hold the pole."

"Your toes on the wheel touch the fork."

"Put your right hand on the saddle and hold onto it."

The first thing you should do is hold onto the saddle while you are mounting. Hold it at the front as shown in the photo. Your other hand should be at your assistant's shoulder. First, step onto the wheel pressing your toes into the fork to block it.

Then, climb up to the lower pedal. As soon as your weight is on it, the wheel can not roll away, even if the assistant doesn't block it for a moment. Move slowly without shaking, so that you do not unbalance the giraffe, and keep your center of gravity close to it.

"Climb slowly onto the lower pedal, and stay close to the pole."

Now, here comes the most difficult part: Take your foot off the wheel, move it over the arms of your assistant, and put it on the upper pedal. It is not necessary to get on the saddle right now. Your assistant may take off one hand at a time to make way for your foot.

"Step carefully over the arm of your assistant, and onto the upper pedal. Don't try to sit down on the saddle yet."

Now, after you have found your balance, you can finally get onto the saddle at last by stepping somewhat more onto the upper pedal a bit to drag yourself up. Hold onto the saddle with one hand, and the shoulder of your assistant with the other. Tell him to keep the wheel blocked. As soon as you sit in the saddle, you should shift your weight, and put about half of it on the pedals again.

"Climb on the saddle and sit down. Shift some weight back on the pedals as soon as possible."

Now, you can take your hand off your assistants shoulder, and take his hand instead. It is your turn to take full control of the giraffe now. Tell your assistant to take the foot away that is in front of your wheel first and then the other one behind your wheel, and then you start idling at once. You will get the hang of it soon because the general feeling is very similar to a normal unicycle.

"At first you take your assistants arm or hand, then he pulls away his feet away – first the one in front of you, and then the other one."

Before you start riding, your pedals should be in the horizontal starting position. Keep your body upright now. You can start idling first or get straight into riding. Your assistant holds his arm up all the time, but he should stay an arms-length away from your giraffe. Since you need some support, he should come along with you.

"You are ready to start. Your assistant holds up one hand all the time, and steps back a bit. Now, you can learn to control the giraffe either by idling or by riding."

"Keep on riding properly all the time. About 3-4 meters is a good distance for beginners."

After you have practiced riding the giraffe with support for a while, it is time to try to ride it on your own. Find some free space where you can reach something to hold onto after riding a short distance. It could be a lamppost or something similar, but make sure it is solid, and can carry your weight. Keep riding properly towards it until you can touch the post without reaching out for it. Don't tilt towards it in the last meter to bridge the gap.

Now, you can turn around at the post and ride back to your assistant or dismount after a few meters (See below: Free mount and dismounting). Learn to ride the giraffe step by step, repeating the same exercises you know from the normal unicycle. Soon you will get used to the new vehicle.

"A lamppost provides excellent support. It is useful for mounting and dismounting when there is no assistant around."

Top right: "Even if you have more than one assistant, they should block the wheel at both sides while you are mounting the giraffe."

Right: "There is an alternative way to mount. Instead of using the wheel as the first step, you can try to step onto the lower pedal at once right away. This way, you need less time to keep the balance."

"Hold the giraffe at the saddle and at the upper pedal. Stand close to the wheel."

"Step onto the lower pedal right away if possible and keep in balance on the other foot as much as possible."

b)   Free Mount and Dismount

Of course, you can mount a giraffe without help as well.

Put it in front of you, and keep a distance of at least 4 meters from any obstacle in all directions. The pedals should be in a vertical position. Hold the upper pedal with one hand, and place the other hand at the front of the saddle (see photo). Now, step on the lower pedal with one huge step.

You can then let go of the upper pedal, and use your hand to steady yourself.

Tilt the giraffe a bit forwards, and move closer to the wheel with the foot you stand upon to get your body as close as possible to the giraffe. Putting enough weight on the lower pedal will prevent the wheel from rolling away from you.

Notice:
If you can not reach the lower pedal with one step because you are simply too short, you can step on the wheel with your **other** foot first. Block the wheel by putting your toes between the fork and the tire. Now you can **reach the lower pedal with your favorite foot.**

"Block the wheel with one foot."

Now, drag yourself up to step on the upper pedal. Keep your center of gravity close to the giraffe at all times. You can even jump up a bit, and get onto the saddle in one smooth movement. As long as you haven't touched the upper pedal yet, you can pull yourself up on the saddle, as well.

Put your weight on both pedals now, and climb over onto the saddle. A low saddle makes it easier to get the saddle between your legs. As soon as you sit properly, you can let go of the saddle. Start idling as soon as you have gained control over the giraffe. This can be even before you actually sit down properly, but then, don't let go of the saddle.

Important:

The trick to successfully mounting a giraffe is to know when the right time to start idling is. If you start idling too early, the saddle might get pushed away from you. Then you will immediately lose control of the giraffe.
If you start idling too late, you may have already fallen to the side too much. It is not possible to then gain your balance again. Tilting forwards or backwards often is less of a problem because you can still try to regain control by riding a bit forwards or backwards.

"Before you try to actually stay on the saddle, practice getting on the upper pedal and on to the saddle, as well as dismounting again several times until you can properly get up and dismount. As soon as you get onto the saddle, start idling. Usually the first idling move is backwards."

There are two ways to dismount: to the front, or to the back. Dismounting to the side is very dangerous, and should be avoided at all costs. Robert recommends dismounting towards the back unless you feel more secure going down forwards.

To dismount towards the back, you should hold the front of the saddle. Don't let it go until you have landed on the floor. Before you dismount, ride more and more slowly and stop pedaling when the pedals are in a vertical position. Take the foot off of the upper pedal, and step backwards a bit. The giraffe stays in front of you all the time, so you can make sure that nobody gets hurt by it, and it doesn't get stuck anywhere as long as you are still on it. Stay on the lower pedal until you can see the wheel in front of you. Just before you touch the floor, you take the other foot off, and try to land with both feet on the floor. You should land upright in the very same place where your giraffe had been shortly before. During the landing, absorb the shock with your knees.

Andreas recommends another way to dismount - getting down forwards:

In order to dismount safely to the front, you again need enough free space **all around you**. Move slowly, and keep your movements under control at all times. Don't simply jump off the giraffe as long as it is still standing. You might lose control entirely, and crash-land on top of the giraffe.

Hold the back of the saddle; stop any pedaling, and let yourself fall forwards slowly with the giraffe, keeping your body tense and upright at the same time (see photo). Now, take the foot off of the upper pedal, and do a very slow and wide step forward.

When you are half-way down, you will feel that the lower pedal is no longer pressing against your lower foot. At this moment, you jump lightly off that second pedal, and land on the floor with both feet simultaneously. Let go of the saddle only if you can not keep your balance after you have landed.

"Do a very slow and long step forward and keep your lower foot on the pedal. You land with both feet simultaneously. Notice that the body stays upright all the time and that just the giraffe tilts forwards."

Be careful: No matter how you dismount, you can not really see what is going on behind you. Someone might have suddenly walked into your path, or you may have passed an obstacle that is now behind you.

If you dismount to the front, your wheel moves backwards, and may strike just such an obstacle. If this happens, the wheel suddenly stops, and the saddle will push hard against your spine throwing you off the giraffe.

This is a disadvantage of mounting forwards. On the other hand, we have found that many people are afraid of dismounting backwards, and therefore, make more mistakes. Make a decision on which way of dismounting you prefer, and then, stick to it. When you dismount, don't mix the movements of the two variations together.

c)   Advanced Techniques on the Giraffe

Generally speaking, anything that is possible on a unicycle can be done on a giraffe, as well: riding backwards, idling, riding standing, jumping rope, riding with one foot, riding on unpaved surfaces, and so on.

Idling is an important technique for anyone to learn who wants to ride a giraffe because if anything obstructs your way, you can stop any time, and idle and ride on instead of dismounting and mounting again.

2 The Ultimate Wheel

a)   Preparations

An Ultimate Wheel is a unicycle without a saddle and a fork.

"An Ultimate Wheel can roll without someone riding it."

With the "drag seat" trick you have already had a chance to explore what it will be like to ride an ultimate. By dismantling the saddle and fork from a normal unicycle, you can create your first ultimate. However, if you know that you really want to learn it, you should buy a proper one. It is much more well-balanced, and thus, easier to ride. You can get more information about equipment in chapter F1c. A very good ultimate is sold by Pichler in Germany **(See retailers in chapter F5)**.

Riding an ultimate is not much more difficult than riding a unicycle but since it behaves quite differently, you have to learn it **like a new technique.** A major difference is of course that you can not put weight on the saddle or use the saddle to change direction.

Important:

Put your weight on both pedals. When one pedal is in the lowest position, all your weight should be on it. There should be just enough weight on the top pedal as you need to keep in contact with it. As you move on, your weight shifts completely to the other side until the pedal in the top position has moved to the lowest position.

Therefore, riding an ultimate resembles walking rather than riding a unicycle. It helps to imagine that you are actually walking on it in a special way, like on a catwalk: your left foot steps across to the right side, and the right foot crosses to the left side. You can first practice this without an ultimate.

"Practice the catwalk without an ultimate."

So for every half turn of your ultimate you have to shift your weight completely from one side to the other. This must be done with great care on the ultimate in order to prevent it from suddenly tilting to one side. Keep your head level at all times, and bend at the knees instead of going up and down with your whole body. Keep your knees bent even if the pedals are level. This way, you can control the ultimate at any time by riding faster or slower. Your legs should be quite tense to move the center of gravity of your body forwards and backwards in order to keep your balance.

Touching the wheel with your calves while riding helps to keep the ultimate under control when it tilts to the side too much. Keep your legs really tense, and close together all the time when the ultimate tilts from one side to the other. As soon as you get the knack of it you can relax a bit.

"It might be a bit strenuous, but well worth the effort to bend at the knees all the time."

"Keep your legs tightly together in the beginning."

The skin of your calves might easily get rubbed raw, so use some protection. Loose-fitting jeans help a lot. They won't rip, move along the tire easily, and they won't get wet with perspiration. If your legs are wet, your skin will get rubbed raw even faster.
Spraying silicon on the wheel reduces the friction a lot. A tire without profile – whether it is a slick or simply an old tire - is also a good idea in any case. More tips on the right equipment can be found in chapter F1c.

b)   Free Mount

To mount the ultimate freely, put it – unlike the unicycle – in front of you with the pedals in an **almost** vertical position! Put your foot on the lower pedal which is a little bit closer to you (see photo). By shifting your weight on it very slowly, you can block the wheel at the top with your leg and it won't tilt or roll backwards. It is not possible to start if the ultimate rolls backwards, so the pedal can't be in the lowest position. As soon as your weight is almost entirely on the pedal, lift your other foot and put it on the upper pedal bending at the knees at the same time.

"The leg against the tire blocks the wheel, and makes sure that it won't move backwards or tilt. By the way, a really good ultimate can indeed be ridden with shorts and without protective clothing."

"Once you move the upper pedal forwards a bit, you can shift some weight on to it bit by bit. You can see that skateboarding shin pads are used here. They come in handy to keep your legs from getting hurt."

In order to start riding, you have to kick the upper pedal a bit forwards with the soles of your shoes without putting much weight on that pedal. If you begin to fall to one side, you can try to remove the weight from that side. Sometimes you then can regain your balance.

Important:

If the ultimate is tilted a bit to the side, you are actually in perfect balance. Your weight on the lower pedal must be in a vertical line **above the tire** in order to keep your balance.

"Control over the ultimate tilting to one side is regained by quickly shifting your weight to the other side. This is only possible if you bend at the knees all the time."

Important tips for riding:

There are **three** possibilities to prevent the ultimate wheel from tilting to one side, which is the greatest difficulty in riding the ultimate. Find the right combination of the different moves for yourself:

- push against the wheel with your leg on the other side (See photo. This is difficult because you will slow down a lot which will make it more difficult in turn to keep your balance. Good equipment is useful in this case.)

- shift your weight to the other pedal using your hips and arms (This also might be tricky because you are shifting your weight constantly anyway when you are riding the ultimate.)

- push against the wheel with your ankle on the other side (see photo. This is an important option, but it will affect your body's balance, as well.)

"Push against the wheel with your ankle to keep your balance. This is only possible with ultimates built from a solid piece of wood."

Now, it is time to practice and finally **enjoy** riding the ultimate!

"Unicyclehockey is a game for everybody!"

D Unicyclehockey
and Other Games, Plus Unicycle Races

1   Unicyclehockey

a)   The Game

Old movies document unicyclehockey games as some kind of theatrical event performed in the 1920s in the *Wintergarten* music hall in Berlin, Germany. Unfortunately, the performers couldn't be identified.

In the 1960s and 70s, unicyclehockey became a team sport in the USA. In 1984, it was introduced in Germany, and within a few years it spread all over the country fascinating an ever-increasing fan base. Then, EDEL (the first German unicyclehockey league) was founded in 1995. Unicyclehockey leagues were also founded in Great Britain and in Switzerland at that time. More than 50 teams compete in the German league today.

Unicyclehockey is a much faster game than unibasketball, and since the hockey sticks can be used to keep your balance while you are idling or riding at the same time, it is easier for beginners, and thus, has become very popular.

Regular hockey sticks can be used for unicyclehockey because a person seated on a unicycle is about as tall as an adult hockey player standing.

Since beginners usually do not play at fixed positions, the stick can be straight and not bent at the end. If it is still too long for you, you can cut off a bit. Short sticks are useful for dribbling, whereas more balls are within your reach with a long stick.

Of course, hitting the ball hard will almost throw you off the unicycle at first, but you will improve quickly. Use both hands on the stick whenever possible.

Even the top teams of the national leagues include girls and boys, as well as, older athletes, and there are also no age groups because unicyclehockey is played as a non-contact sport. The rules are very easy. Together with some tips for unicyclehockey referees, you can find the rules in detail on **www.einradhockeyliga.de**. This is the homepage of the German unicyclehockey league.

b)   Key Rules

Having fun is most important. All equipment you use should be kept in good condition. Here is a short outline of the rules to give you an idea of the game. You can download the complete set of rules from www.einradhockey.de.

The teams should agree on a set of rules depending on the space available and the players' age and skill levels.

- Unicyclehockey is a game for everyone: girls and boys, old and young, beginners and advanced riders.

- Use hockey sticks (not the special goal keeper type) and an old tennis ball and small goals.

- The upper end of the stick should be covered with one hand at all times for safety. The lower end must be held lower than your hip. Make sure that you don't hurt anyone with your stick in particular before or after shooting.

- If player A holds his stick so that player B rides over the stick (or gets the stick into his spokes) then player A has fouled player B (called "SUB") no matter if it was intentional or not.

- A player may take part in the game only as long as he is on his unicycle. If someone has to dismount, he has to stay where he is and mount again. As long as he is not on his unicycle, he has to dodge other players and the ball.

- At the start and after each goal, all players return to their half of the field until the ball or one player has crossed the middle line.

- You may touch the ball with your open hand once, but you can not score a goal this way.

- Throwing the stick deliberately is a foul.

- A goal shot from beyond the middle line must be touched by someone on the other side before it can count.

If no real hockey goals are available, of course, you can improvise.

We started with toppled shopping carts on a parking lot. Ideally, the field should be about 35-45m long and 20-25m wide. There should be a barrier all around the sides, and the corners should be round.

It doesn't matter if someone holds onto the goal at the beginning, but you should try to learn idling as soon as possible. A team is made of five players, but in small sport halls fewer players are sometimes better. You should wear shoes, and keep your laces short. Earrings, rings, watches, and necklaces should be removed before the game.

Tip:

Make sure that not all of you chase after the ball. Spread across the field a bit. All players should see that the other players follow the rules because all of you are responsible that no one gets hurt.

It is preferable of course, to play with a referee because he can judge fouls better, for instance, sticks being held improperly, or a stick swung too high.

In the league, we play with two or even more referees. The referees shouldn't concentrate on the ball too much (the ball doesn't hurt anyone) but instead on the players and the sticks. In order to keep the game under control, the referee shouldn't be on a unicycle.

2 Other Great Games on the Unicycle

Many games you know from school or Kindergarten, as well as many team sports like basketball or handball can be played on unicycles. Simply adapt the difficulty level to the players' skills, and experiment with changing a few rules.

Just have fun on the unicycle, and find new challenges.

To prepare your unicycle for a game, make sure that there are no sharp edges at the pedals or the seat bolt. Tape them if necessary.

Below, we recommend a few games we have tested.

"Who is Afraid of the Troll?"

This classic variation of "Catch Me if You Can" can be played on the unicycle very well. It is easy to play, many players can be involved, and it needs no great preparation. All you need are players who can ride reasonably well and a space big enough.

One player (not a beginner if possible) starts on one side. The rest are in one line on the opposite side. The single player is the "troll" who calls, "Who is afraid of the troll?" The rest answer, "No one!" Then, the "troll" asks, "But what if he comes?" and the rest reply, "Then, we will ride away!" At that time, they start to ride to the opposite side, trying to escape the "troll." All who have been touched by the troll on their way to the other side are trolls the next time, as well. Those who have reached the other side are safe for that round.

In the next round, all trolls try to catch the remaining free players until all have been caught. The last one who is caught is the troll in the next game.

Chasing

All players ride in a line, one behind the other. The first one performs a trick or a special movement like crossing his arms behind his back, or bending down, and all the others have to imitate him. Then, the first player leaves the top position, and follows the last player in the line.

"Fisherman, Fisherman How Deep is the Water?"

This game is similar to the one above, but it is more like a competition. It is a good opportunity to combine playing a game with some tricks on the unicycle. However, you need a big space. One player, who is the fisherman, is at one side, the others are on the other side. They call, "Fisherman, fisherman, how deep is the water?" The fisherman decides how deep it is, and tells them, "It is 42m deep!" The others call, "How do we get to the other side then?" The fisherman tells them what they have to do – which trick they have to perform – to get to the other side, for instance, riding backwards or with one leg. All players who can't do the trick, or who fall off their unicycle trying it may be touched by the fisherman, and become fishermen themselves. All players who get to the other side performing the trick remain free, and may start a new round.

It is not necessary that the fisherman must be able to perform the trick himself while chasing the other players. This depends on the skill level of the players. Decide this before you start playing.

There is no need to choose difficult tricks at the beginning. Riding with one hand on your back, or with one eye closed is sufficient for a start.
The last free player in the game is the fisherman in the next game.

Catching
Many variations of catching games can be played on the unicycle: in pairs, in chains, etc.

Variation on Musical Chairs
There are a number of unicycles on the floor, but always one less than the number of participants. A neutral person starts the music. As long as the music is playing, the players run around the pile of unicycles. Once the music stops, the players try to grab a unicycle, and ride it. If one unicycle is claimed by more than one player, they may try to ride it together. The record in this game is six players on one unicycle. Anyone who is not able to claim a unicycle is out. Then, the music starts again, and the players dismount, and return the unicycles to the middle of the room. One (or more) of the unicycles is taken away by the neutral person until only one remains.

A very funny variation is to manipulate the unicycles a bit. A saddle or a pedal can be removed or fixed at an unusual angle, tires can be deflated, and so on.

The Atom-game
All the unicyclists ride around. A neutral person calls out a number between the number "one" and the number of players playing. As soon as the players have heard the number called out, they try to build groups with as many members as that number. Those who can not build a group are out, either until the next round, or until the end of the game.

Riding and Guessing Letters or Numbers
One player thinks of a letter, and in principle, writes the letter on the floor by using the tire of his unicycle as a pencil, in effect, "riding out" the letter without telling the other players which one it is. The others try to guess which letter of the alphabet it is. The player who gets it right may "ride" the next letter.

Slalom
Who can ride the closest slalom without mistakes ?

Slow Ride
Who can take the longest to ride a distance of about 10-30 m? Jumping, freezing, idling or riding backwards is not allowed. Turning to the side too much is also not allowed. The best way to play this game is to ride between two lines about 30-50cm apart.

Mounts per Minute
Who can mount, hop, idle, kick-up, or ride a circle the most times in one minute?

Relay Races
Which team wins the relay race? It is funnier and more challenging when the relay is ridden carrying funny items like hats or chairs, or riding while carrying them in a certain posture.

Races of Any Kind
Make sure that you wear some protective gear, and play fair.

Chain
How many unicyclists does it take to build the longest chain? (See page 108.)

Blind Date
One player closes his eyes while riding on a large free space. His partner rides nearby telling him where to go, or calling him over, or directing him to follow. Naturally, some responsibility rests on the one who is directing.

Circuit Training
You set up a circuit training course with different stations. Exercises for unicyclehockey like shooting, cornering, passing, and so on can be practiced. Tricks on the unicycle are also possible stations: mounting, riding backwards, wheel walking, etc.

According to the skill level of the participants, the tricks can get more and more difficult. Circuit training should be fun; however, more importantly, it is a good opportunity to practice different techniques.

Gladiator or Highlander

In a limited enclosed area, all unicyclists try to stay on the unicycle as long as possible. Those who have to dismount are out and leave the space. The last one riding has won. It is not allowed to pull clothes, hit, bite or do anything that would hurt the other players. However, obstructing the way, leaning or nudging others is acceptable.
A variation would be to use plastic bags filled with hay to hit each other.

Sumo

This game can be pedagogically used to transform aggression into skillful riding. It is played very often on unicycle meetings like the UNICON. A circle of 3-4m diameter is drawn on the floor. A referee should be present to make sure that the game is played fair. There are always only two unicyclists within the circle. They play the game "Gladiator or Highlander" (see above). The player who has to dismount or leave the circle loses. The winner is challenged by the next contender. There is no final winner. Take it as a funny personal challenge.

Softball

This is easily adapted from the traditional game. The players (in the field) should be able to pick up the ball from the floor or play without a unicycle here. At the home base, you can idle or dismount and mount again. Placing obstacles between the bases may increase the fun.

Volleyball (also known as Volleywheel among unicyclists)

This game can be adapted very easily, but you will soon realize how slow you are on the unicycle. In order to get the game going, you should decide whether the ball may bounce on the floor once or even twice, according to the skill level of the players.

Basketball

This game has been played very often already and there is a tournament on each UNICON. Very successful teams come from Puerto Rico, the Netherlands, and the USA, as well as from France and Switzerland. Up until now, all world champions have come from Puerto Rico or the Netherlands.

It is required that at least one player on each team can pick up the ball from the floor. The rules are very easy to adapt. It is not permitted to touch the ball with your unicycle. Basketball on the unicycle was very popular (in Germany) in the 1990s, but today, the faster paced unicyclehockey is usually played instead.

Tour

How about a day tour on the unicycle? Take some food, and drink with you. A small daypack poses no problem, does it?

3 Unicycle Races

The bigger your wheel is in diameter and the shorter the cranks are, the faster you can ride on a unicycle. For obvious reasons, wheels and cranks should, therefore, have certain standard dimensions in a race. In Switzerland, there have been races since the 1970ies, and in the 1990ies races with 26" size wheels were very popular. Although these races were the first ones in Europe, and although the 26" size wheel was very common for artistic bicycle riding, today, the 26" wheels are no longer very common in races.

Usually in national and international competitions, a minimum length of 125mm for cranks and a maximum size of the wheel of 24,333" (61,8 cm) are allowed.
There are also races for children under ten years of age, where a maximum size of 20,333" for the wheel, and a minimum length of 102mm for the cranks are mandated.

Pedals with straps and click-pedals are prohibited, as well.
The power of your feet must be transmitted directly to the wheel, so no additional means of power transmission are allowed. For the German Marathon Championships in Düsseldorf, a 28"-wheel is used and the crank has to be at least 104 cm long. With that combination of wheel-size and crank, you wouldn't normally ride in the streets for fun because you couldn't stop within one turn of the wheel. Riding uphill and downhill and turning corners is a problem, as well, with these unicycles. Yet if you ride in a well organized marathon, you don't have to bother about pedestrians suddenly crossing your way. Since you need a specially constructed unicycle, only a comparatively small number of unicyclists take part in this competition. By the way, riding in a marathon is less strenuous than running.

Equipment Tips

Usually, races take place outdoors. Since you do not know what the weather will be like, you should be prepared for all possible weather conditions. Your pedals should have good contact to your shoes even if both are wet. A large pedal with tiny spikes and shoes with soles of soft rubber and a good profile may help a lot.
The cross section of your tire should be rounded which helps you to grip the road when you turn corners. A course tread is useful for riding cross-country, of course, but on a racetrack, you might easily drift to the side with it. Maximum tire pressure helps to reduce the friction between the wheel and the ground. The maximum

amount of air can be pumped into a tire that has been stored lying flat, in order to avoid the tire becoming misshapen, in a dark basement with enough fresh air, and it must be protected from direct sunlight, or otherwise the tire will become brittle. After a year in such conditions, all substances that soften a tire will have evaporated.

The lighter your unicycle is the faster you can accelerate. If rim and tire are heavier, you have more weight in motion once you have achieved enough speed. This means that it is harder to accelerate, but the unicycle runs more smoothly at a high rate of speed. It depends on your maximum speed and the length of the race wether a heavier wheel is useful or not.

Aerodynamic resistance is not very important on a unicycle since it is dependent upon the speed. You will simply not get fast enough to feel a significant aerodynamic resistance.

Wind coming from the side, however, is a problem since you have to be careful to keep your balance.

Whether a handle on your saddle is useful or not, depends on your style of riding.

Tips on Riding Technique

Steady and even pedaling will make you faster than sporadic pedaling. Struggling to keep your balance because of side wind, or because you have to turn a corner will also slow you down.

So practice pedaling steadily and evenly. Some of you may have learned this technique already on a bike with click-pedals. Here the pedals are not only pushed down in front but also pulled up behind, so much more momentum is gained. You can not do exactly the same thing on a unicycle, but the principle still holds good.

Your feet should transfer the momentum to the pedals as long as possible in each turn. This can only be done with your ankles working hard. Your feet do not only push down the pedal in front of you, but in the top position of one pedal they push it forward a bit and in the lowest position they pull them backwards a bit.

Once you are going really fast, this is not possible anymore, but at the start, it helps a lot to accelerate. Practice this while you are riding slowly. Find out which posture helps your speed to increase. There are postures which allow you to gain some extra speed, but you have to keep in mind that some of them make it hard to keep your balance.

"German Championship Races 2005"

Robert bends his upper body forward quite a lot. It looks like he is trying to reduce the air friction, but in fact he is just keeping his balance this way.

Most of the other unicyclists are riding upright and tilt forwards some with the whole body.

They press one or both hands on the front top of the saddle (an additional grip makes this easier) and put some weight on it to move their center of gravity forwards a bit. This helps a little in gaining speed, but it has to be practiced, as well.

Many unicyclists use this method for the final sprint, and try to gain a fraction of a second at the finishing line by falling forward. The time is usually recorded when the front of your unicycle "crosses" the finishing line, but you get disqualified if your unicycle is no longer under your control when the hub of it crosses the line.

So don't jump off the unicycle at the end. However, there may be variations of these rules at different championships. Sometimes the whole unicycle has to cross the line before you may jump off it. Ask for the house rules before you take part in a race.

Before You Start:
Check if your cranks are fixed tightly. Are any other screws loose? Is the tire pressure correct? Is your protective gear complete and properly fitted? Are your shoelaces tied and short enough? Do you have your start number on, and can it be seen properly? Listen to the announcements, and if your start number has been called, get ready to start.

The Start:
The countdown usually is: "Get ready - ready – steady – go!", or "1-2-3-go!", or "3-2-1-go!" The intervals of time between the four steps are equal, so you can anticipate the start, and prepare yourself by tilting forward just before the start. This is allowed as long as your wheel stays behind the starting line. Start posts help you to keep your balance while standing, and you may use them also to push yourself away at the start. Remember to pedal steadily and evenly especially at the beginning. The sooner you reach your maximum speed the better.

The Race:
Plan your race well according to your stamina. Are you a good sprinter? Then, it might be a good idea to ride a bit slower in the middle part of the race. Try to ride the shortest path, but stay at least one wheel's length away from other competitors.

Don't lose your rhythm, and don't struggle just because someone else overtakes you. If you fall off the unicycle, you will lose the chance for a top position in the race.

Robert has won a whole lot of races because other competitors tried to keep pace with him when he overtook them, but they fell off their unicycle instead. They lost everything in that moment, and Robert could finish the race easily.

"This is the official obstacle course of the IUF (International Unicycle Federation). It is an invariant part of any IUF championship."

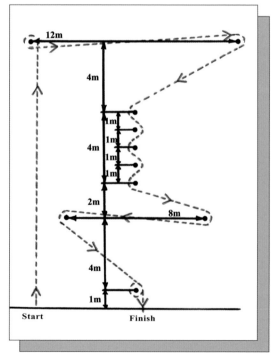

"In a perfect turn, your head is exactly above the cone."

In the obstacle course, the race is not directly against other competitors rather against the clock. Every single competitor is timed like in a ski race. A regular rhythm is most important here. Prepare your turns early enough. When riding through the cones in a line, ideally your head should follow a straight line above the cones (while the unicycle sways around them). Your wheel turns and your hips control the unicycle. You may touch the cones (30cm x 30cm, 45-60 cm high) but not topple them.

E How to Teach Unicycling

1 Preliminary Considerations

The following chapter is intended for teachers and instructors, but it also offers useful information for interested (adult) beginners on ways to learn how to improve the experience while learning to ride a unicycle.

a)   Comparing the Movement Patterns of the Unicycle, the Bike, and Walking

Unicycling resembles walking in many respects. It is less similar to riding a bike, however. On a bike, most of the weight rests on the saddle, and you can tilt or bend forward and backward without it affecting your balance.

On a bike, you can mount without standing firmly on both pedals, and you don't have to keep contact with them while you ride it. Neither is possible when you learn to ride a unicycle. If you tried, the unicycle would suddenly roll away from underneath you.

A good exercise is to ride a bike using click-pedals, and practice smooth, round pedaling with constant contact to the pedals.

Timid beginners dismount or jump off the unicycle (long) before they have actually lost their balance. Transferring the knowledge of how to ride a bike, they put too much weight on the saddle in order to be able to take their feet off the pedals, and put them back on the floor as quickly as possible. This behavior obstructs the learning process a lot. Only if you stay on the unicycle for long enough, do you have the chance to get the proper feel for it, and learn something.

Of course, beginners can fall from the unicycle and hurt themselves more easily if they try to stay on the unicycle even if they have problems at that moment with keeping their balance.

But you have to take that risk if you want to learn something!

On the other hand, you should avoid any pointless risks (see chapter A 2b).

Unicycling is like a constant controlled falling movement; the feeling it creates in your stomach can be compared to floating in the air above the floor, and this feeling is a great reward for the hard work you had to put into learning it.

b)   Purpose

Two main **objectives** can be distinguished resulting from two different traditions of unicycling. For more than 100 years, the unicycle has been part of the European Kunstradsport or Artistic Sport-cycling. This tradition dates back to the time when the bicycle and unicycle were invented simultaneously, and the focus is more on technique and athletics although the artistic aspect is important, as well. Competitions and elaborate costumes are important here. Although Artistic Sport-cycling dates further back, it played a lesser role in the recognition of unicycling as a popular sport.

A more playful approach has been taken by groups of children rehearsing circus performances and by young jugglers. Unicycling and juggling complement one another since one requires control over the upper body, and the other one over the lower body.

The kids and young jugglers approached the unicycle in a more casual, free, and informal way. They cared less about rules, and sometimes got hurt badly when they practiced their unorthodox methods.

These people have helped a lot to spread unicycling as a playful sport.
    But, in fact, it took the cooperation of both traditions to promote the incredible success of the unicycle over the last few years.

There are also different ways of learning how to unicycle. The methods may be totally different, and yet, still very successful at the same time.

At the beginning of this book, we explained to you how to learn how to ride the unicycle. We said that the beginner should put all his weight on the pedals because this gives him the best control over the unicycle. This is fully true, and yet you can learn it the other way around just as well: If you sit on the saddle with all your weight on it and almost no weight on the pedals (just enough to keep in contact with them at all times) you can learn from the beginning how to ride the unicycle with great ease. With this method, an instructor must point out to any learner that he should sit properly on the saddle.

It is, in fact, easier to ride a unicycle this way because you are sitting rather than standing all the time. For people who weigh more than most, or for those who tend to get muscle aches, or simply for adults this method can be better. Some beginners might also feel that this method is easier. Smooth, rounded pedaling is of the greatest importance here. Many other basic principles of how to keep your balance remain exactly the same. Skilled unicyclists should be able to freely shift their weight between saddle and pedals anyway, depending on which trick or technique they perform at that moment.

About fifteen years ago, just as many boys as girls rode the unicycle. Today, it is favored by girls from 7-14 years, in particular, and by a few very successful boys from 14-19 years of age. The girls who start unicycling are also much younger today. This affects the methods of how unicycling is best taught a lot. Most young girls learn it simply by watching those who can already ride. Explanations should be kept to a minimum. It is better to correct anything that is actually done improperly than to say in advance what is important. You can help younger kids most by supporting them while they ride (see A1b) and motivating them constantly with praise. Since young children learn mostly by copying, watching others doing it well is the most important part of the learning process.

Young kids on a unicycle tend to ride it for hours. Often they lack motivation or simply the imagination to learn more than simple riding. For us teachers, it is important to show them that there is more to unicycling than just "moving forward and not falling from the unicycle." Once you have seen how much can be achieved on the unicycle, you are motivated to go on. At about 10-11 years of age, children are again more interested in advanced techniques, and it is easier to teach them.

The biomechanical aspects of unicycling, like how to keep the forces in balance when mounting, can only be explained to older unicyclists, of course.

All unicyclists should meet every now and then in order to learn together and share experiences. This creative pool is necessary to really excel at the difficult techniques. So, come to the national and international meetings and conventions (see chapter F) as often as possible to meet hundreds of fellow unicyclists who share your interests. The UNICON, the world championship, is organized by the International Unicycle Federation (IUF) and takes place every two years in a different country.

Of course, the internet has become a very important medium for unicyclists, as well. Many clips with incredible tricks at all skill levels can be easily downloaded. Some interesting homepages are mentioned in chapter F 4.

c)   Recommendations for Teaching Methods

Riding in pairs is much easier than riding alone. Both unicyclists don't have to be very skilled, but they should have a clue of how to stay on the unicycle. Over the short periods of time when they need support, their partner is probably not in trouble himself, and can help them keep their balance.

Riding in pairs is very effective, in particular when you learn riding backwards. One is riding backwards, the other one forwards looking in opposite directions. They hold one or both of each others hands. After a few meters, they can change direction, swapping roles.

Put your right hands and left hands together. This is a reliable combination for two people. It offers you a wide range of possibilities. Both unicyclists support each other so first exercises can be performed successfully, and this motivates them to continue. While riding, both or one of the unicyclists can change directions by turning around without changing the hand position or affecting the other unicyclist too much. Try circles and riding backwards, as well. The assistant is not walking at your side, but is integrated into the exercise itself, and can enjoy it, as well.

Put together a short routine if you want. At first, you can walk the sequence without the unicycle instead of riding it. Keep in mind that the pedals need some space, so keep enough distance on all sides. This is also very useful in learning how not to misjudge what you can actually do on a unicycle, like how much space you really need to turn around.

"In pairs you can head into the same direction or into opposite directions."

"With both hands holding both hands, you can turn around and change the direction without having to tell your partner beforehand."

Not only can you ride in pairs, but also in long chains. For the less experienced, this is a possibility to participate in an easy formation. The first step to learn the chain is to learn the mount together. At first, this takes a lot of practice and patience from all participants, but the reward is great. Suddenly, everyone will have learned it together simultaneously, and a feeling of great team spirit spreads.

If you want to perform a chain successfully, all participants should prepare their pedals correctly, and experienced unicyclists and beginners should alternate in the chain. Then, one after the other starts to mount their unicycle until each has mounted.

"The chain is a hard test for all participants, but the reward is great, as well."

A variation which can be performed only with a really large number of participants is the circle. In this formation, there is no beginning and no end which helps a lot. All start with the same posture. Hold up your hands a bit, and keep your arms and hands somewhat tense. Don't blame others for any faults! There are two reasons for this: First of all, what you say may be wrong because all participants affect each other, and it is very hard to tell who is responsible for what. In addition, if all the kids talk simultaneously, they can not listen to the instructor who is not on a unicycle himself and who can see the whole group and better spot the real problem. So, it is a good idea to tell all participants that at first they shouldn't talk at all, instead they should listen to any instruction.

A chain (but not a circle) can start to ride together! They can ride forwards, backwards, split, reunite, and even stand still.

d) Public Transportation and Unicycles

In different countries the rules are different. In Germany, the unicycle is not mentioned expressis verbis in the Highway Code. Therefore, it is classified as a toy like a skateboard or a kickboard, and you may not use it in public traffic. Some unicyclists take the view that a unicycle that is equipped with lights, a bell, reflectors, brakes and everything else a bike needs in order to be classified as safe, may be used in public traffic just like a bike, but this is not true. You may impress a police officer with it, and even show him that you are a responsible person, but it is still not allowed. Strictly speaking, you are not even supposed to ride on bike paths, but most people will probably accept you riding there. Remember that even a pedestrian zone is not meant to be a playground for unicycles. Inform yourself about how bikes and skateboards are seen in different regions, and try to adapt your behavior accordingly.

"Practice riding forwards while looking back over your shoulder."

A good exercise (that will impress your parents, as well) is to look back over your shoulder while riding. Ride along a straight line while your assistant follows at your side a few meters behind. He can even be on a unicycle himself. Now, he holds up a certain number of fingers, and you have to tell him how many there are by looking backwards without stopping while you are trying to stay on the straight line.

Practice looking backwards over both shoulders. Your assistant shows a different numbers of fingers each time, and he can also vary his position behind you. He starts diagonally behind you, and finishes directly behind you, or even beyond the line you are riding along thus, making you turn back even more than 180°.

"If the passageway for the conductor on a train is obstructed by unicycles, you may get into trouble."

Up until now in many countries, unicycles were not mentioned in the price schedules of train companies. It is not necessary to buy a ticket meant for a bike because that ticket is only for proper bikes. This doesn't mean, on the other hand, that you do not have to pay a fee for the unicycle. In the end, the conductor has the right to decide whether you may take a unicycle with you or not. For 20" unicycles, this is not a problem anyway because they easily fit below the seats or into the luggage rack. A 24" unicycle can be easily put in the aisle even on long distance trains if you make sure that no one gets hurt, in particular, by the pedals. Bigger unicycles and giraffes sometimes cause bigger problems. You can put a giraffe upright and lean it against any wall for a short journey. Make sure that nothing gets caught between the chain and the cogwheel. It helps if you hold the pedal with one hand and turn the chain towards your body. Sometimes it is a very good idea to unscrew the pedal(s). Normally, you just have to cover the unicycle with something, and people will not be aware that it is actually there. Your sleeping bag is perfect to cover a giraffe on a long journey, but a large plastic bag is just as useful. I go into the special bike compartment if the train has one. There, you usually don't have to explain the presence of your unicycle.

"The unicycle can be easily combined with juggling and other circus techniques."

2 Challenges and Elaborate Tricks

a) Combinations and Acrobatics on the Unicycle

In order to make the most of your unicycle, and to be able to offer something to groups who include skilled unicyclists, you should be constantly on the look out for further new challenges. Combinations with other circus techniques may help to broaden your repertoire. Some possibilities have already been mentioned above of which techniques can be combined with the unicycle: picking things up from the floor, jumping rope, balancing on a beam, etc.

Juggling and unicycling is a great combination, and almost a natural one. The unicycle is controlled with the feet, legs, and hips, whereas juggling is done with the arms and upper body. Putting both together is an ideal combination. In order to perform two different techniques together, you should start them one by one. Start with the unicycle because then you can do the difficult mount first. Keep your juggling props ready in your hand, and start juggling as soon as your unicycle is under control.

111

Split up your concentration between all your various activities. This requires the ability to decentralize your concentration, and trains your peripheral perception a lot.

Juggling or acrobatics – like jumping rope – have to first be learned without the unicycle, of course. This can be done with the help of books (see F4) or by being instructed by some experienced jugglers or acrobats. You can go to one of their meetings in any good size city (information on how to find them is published in the European juggling magazine "Cascade" or any other international juggling magazine, see F4).

Two people on one unicycle is not as difficult as you might think, in particular if the one who is riding it is very skilled in idling and used to riding with some extra weight. The best position is to sit on the shoulders or to ride piggy-back. But it is also possible to stand on the fork, on the thighs close to the belly, or put your hands on the shoulders of the rider.

Can you ride with all four feet on the pedals? Or can both of you sit on the saddle?

"Stand on the fork, on the thighs close to the body, or sit on the shoulders. Find out more possibilities to ride one unicycle together."

b) The Rating of Skill Levels

There is an official rating of skill levels for freestyle performances in unicycle championships similar to figure skating or free-style skiing. A complete list can be found, e.g. under www.rad-net.de , but we personally do not believe in such a strict and bureaucratic categorization since it depends largely on individual skills if you find something difficult or not.

In this book, we have roughly rated the difficulty of the tricks and skills in order to show you if you have to expect more or less difficulties when you try to learn it.

Next to the chapter headings you will find one to three icons to show you the skill level.

 = Skill level 1

 = Skill level 2

 = Skill level 3

"The more icons that are next to the chapter headings the more difficulties you can expect."

We think that you can only talk about skill levels properly once you have learned to ride the unicycle even if this may have been difficult in itself, so riding forwards can be considered as skill level 0.

Skill level 1 is everything that is about as difficult as idling, riding backwards or as riding forwards in a special way (like riding on a plank or over gravel).
Skill level 2 is as difficult as a variation of idling, and skill level 3 is simply a bit more difficult, but it can be learned nevertheless! It just may take a few weeks to learn it.

F All About the Unicycle
Equipment, Links, and Retailers

1 Equipment and Tips for Buying Your Unicycle

a) Unicycles

What You Should Know When You Buy a Unicycle

Let's make one thing clear from the start: a unicycle is not half of a bike. The spare parts and the main components of a unicycle are not available in bicycle shops because they differ from bicycle material. There is no handle-bar on a unicycle, and the saddle of a bike also wouldn't be very helpful. Early models of unicycles used bike saddles that were tilted a bit but this was, naturally, quite uncomfortable.

The hub of a unicycle has to be specially manufactured because it is fixed to the cranks and the wheel at the same time. This is the main difference between a bicycle and a unicycle. On a unicycle, you also won't find the cranks of a bike because the crank of a bike is fixed to the cogwheel which moves the chain.

All of these special constructions make a unicycle different from the mass-produced, omnipresent bike. Unicycles are still produced only in small numbers, and are more expensive than you might expect. In China, Taiwan, Japan and some other parts of Asia, the unicycle is a popular children's toy and can, therefore, be found in many schools where it is used during recess for recreation and fun. It is produced in large quantities there, but only for Asian kids and for adults who are, in general, a bit smaller than Europeans. These reasonably priced unicycles from Asia are often not as solid as desired. They are often sold in supermarkets, and by mail order companies. They also appear more and more frequently in internet auctions and shops specializing in unicycles; they usually offer them as a cheaper and more viable alternative to the expensive brands.

Today, there is a well established market for unicycles, and many new manufacturers are in competition with each other. Almost on a daily basis, new models appear while others disappear. Therefore, in order to avoid becoming quickly outdated, we refrain from recommending any specific brands, rather we tell you what to look for, in general, when buying a unicycle. A well-informed retailer will be able to tell you which individual unicycle meets your requirements if you are able to tell him specifically what you are looking for.

There are many variations of unicycles within a wide range of prices. The wheel size varies between 12 and 50 inches.

Important:

The most expensive unicycle is not necessarily the ideal unicycle for you.
Smaller wheels are not automatically appropriate for smaller people.

Think about what you want to do with the unicycle. The following suggestions might help you decide. Below you will find a list which might help you decide which unicycle suits your individual needs best. First, think about what you want to do with the unicycle.

- I just want to try it.

- I want to learn how to ride a unicycle and do some tricks.

- I want to ride on the streets, maybe together with some friends.

- I want to ride long distances, maybe even races.

- I can already ride a unicycle, and I want to learn more: some difficult tricks, to ride longer distances or cross country.

- I want to do acrobatics on the unicycle.

- I want to play hockey on the unicycle.

A General Recommendation for Buying Your First Unicycle:
Although many characteristics of a unicycle are not strictly good or bad, but rather suitable or not suitable for you, it is possible to recommend a kind of "standard unicycle" for a 10 year-old kid. 20" or 24" wheels are best to learn how to ride because with this size, cycling most resembles the walking movement in both speed and extension. 16" wheels are used only by children who are too small to ride a 20" unicycle when the saddle is in its lowest position. Wheels that are bigger than 24" are not suitable for beginners. Of course, 24" unicycles can be used to play hockey, and with

16" wheels you can ride cross country, but it is not the best choice for a general, all-purpose unicycle. It may also be important whether one of your friends already has a unicycle, and if you want to do tricks or tours together. In this case, we recommend the same size of wheels. Otherwise, one of you is in a hurry all the time whereas the other one, in the meantime, is bored.

Before you buy a unicycle, you should also study the passages in this chapter on saddles, saddle poles, seat clamps and cranks. The following recommendation will tell you what to look for starting with the most important aspects.

Your first unicycle could look like this:
A 20" wheel, ball bearings held in shells, at least 28 spokes, a seat clamp with an Allen Key®, a hard saddle with extra plastic protection at the front and back of the saddle fixed with screws, rubber coated pedals, and a tire in a light color if you want to ride indoors.

We doubt that a unicycle with these exact specifications is readily for sale anywhere. Nevertheless, the first four aspects are very important, and you should pay attention to them. Of course, it depends a lot on how much you want to spend on your unicycle. A beginner unicycle should cost no more than 70 € /75 $ / 50 GBP. **For 50 € / 55 $ / 35 GBP, you can already get a proper unicycle** these days. In a unicycle specialty shop, you can customize the unicycle, picking all of the parts out separately according to your wishes and then buy it, but this is more expensive, of course.

If you have already bought a unicycle, then you should first check whether the pedals are fixed on the correct sides. Sometimes, they are screwed on incorrectly by people in shops who do not specialize in unicycles. The pedals are marked with "R"(right) and "L" (left) and the cranks show the same marks. Read pages 143- 144 for more information.

The saddle is fixed in its position with the seat clamp. The way to determine the right height of the saddle is the same as it is on a bike. If you sit properly on the saddle, you should be able to reach the pedals with the soles of your shoes without fully stretching your legs out.
   Sharp edges of screws and other metal pieces are best covered with tape for safety reasons.

If you have made up your mind to only use your unicycle for some special purpose, and if you are thinking of buying a second unicycle, the following table might be helpful to you.

This is what I want to do:	Recommended unicycle:	Pros and cons:	Where to get it:	Average price in $ US
Just learn to ride it, maybe do some tricks later	20", square fork	More agile with its small wheel	Everywhere where unicycles are sold	$50 to 90 in specialty shops up to $130
Just learn to ride it, maybe some long distance rides later	24"	Faster and better for uneven surfaces with its bigger wheel	Everywhere where unicycles are sold the whole year	$90 to 150
Unicyclehockey	20", for agility	No special unicycle needed	Everywhere where unicycles are sold	$90 to 150
Long distances	28", special cranks according to distance and route	Fast unicycle, but you sit quite high above the ground	John Foss, Siegmono	$250 to 380
Official championship competitions	24" (61,8cm diameter), rubber pedals, 125mm cranks	Faster than 20", less suitable for tricks	Everywhere where unicycles are sold the whole year, make sure that the cranks have the officially required length	$90 to 380 the more expensive the lighter (and better) it should be

This is what I want to do:	Recommended unicycle:	Pros and cons:	Where to get it:	Average price in $ US
Tricks (Freestyle) on the streets	20", square fork, good hub, handle on the saddle, rather short cranks, high tire-pressure tires, light colored tires for gymnasiums	Agile, light	Several juggling shops, Municycle.com, Ajata, Siegmono; (see chapter F5)	$150 to 380
Trial (stairs and jumps)	Trial, MUni 20", square fork, good hub, multi-cog hub would be great, handle on the saddle, wide tire	Good for jumping; spare parts available only from specialty shops	Municycle.com, Ajata, Several juggling shops,	$320 to 650 as a rule of thumb: the more expensive the more durable
MUni (Mountain Unicycle) for cross country (see photo page 128)	MUni 24", square fork, good hub, handle on the saddle, wide tire, long cranks,	Good for cross country, spare parts only available from specialty shops	Several juggling shops, Municycle.com, Ajata,	$320 to 650 as a rule of thumb: the more expensive the more durable it is

This is what I want to do:	Recommended unicycle:	Pros and cons:	Where to get it:	Average price in $ US
Acrobatics	20", square fork, good hub, handle on the saddle, wide tire or high tire pressure	Solid and light	Pichler	$380 to 650
Juggling on the unicycle	20", rather long cranks	Slow idling possible	Everywhere where unicycles are sold	$50 to 90; in specialty shops up to $130

This is what I want to do:	Other wheel size:	Pros and cons:	Where to get it:	Average price in $ US
Fun, street performance	12"	Strenuous to ride	Siegmono, Pappnase, Pichler, juggling shops;	$320
For smaller kids	16"	More expensive	Siegmono, juggling shops	$60 to 120
For smaller kids	18"	Few spare parts available	Siegmono	$100 to 130
Compromise between 20" and 24" (see above)	22"	Few spare parts available	Siegmono	$130

This is what I want to do:	Other wheel size:	Pros and cons:	Where to get it:	Average price in $ US
Longer distances	26"	Feel similar to 24", few spare parts available	Siegmono, Municycle.com	
Longer distances	29", 30"	Less strenuous, few spare parts available	Siegmono, Municycle.com, Pichler	
Long distances, open straight streets	36"+	High momentum uphill/downhill, hard to accelerate/brake	Pappnase, Municycle.com	$380 to 750
Show	Giraffe	Very effective	Siegmono, juggling shops, internet	Less than $150; but you should invest at least $250; special giraffes may cost a lot more
Show	Giraffe	Very effective, very durable and reliable	Pichler	$380 and more; customized constructions possible

This is what I want to do:	Other wheel size:	Pros and cons:	Where to get it:	Average price in $ US
Show and challenge	Twice (a second wheel on top of the first, so it's driven backwards)	Hard to ride	Siegmono, Pichler	$380
Show	Three Wheeler (three wheels on top of each other – the driver moves forward)	Really heavy	Siegmono, Pichler	$560
Show, challenge	Ultimate	Not dangerous, yet quite impressive	Municycle.com, Pichler, DM	$130 to 250
Challenge, fun	Kangaroo (both pedals to the front, hub not centered)	Funny variation	Assembly required with a normal hub, Ask for it at any specialty shops	depends on the shop
Challenge	Impossible (the feet balance on an extended axle)	Hard to ride	Municycle.com; Ask for it	$150

If you are a beginner, don't be afraid of this long list with expensive prices: The suggestions are intended for people who already have one or two unicycles, and are looking for something special. Nevertheless, it is just a rough outline. Good shops will have even more different unicycles in stock. Considering the current success of unicycles, the variety will probably even increase over time.

Unicycles from Vitelli and Imholz are not mentioned in this list although they are well-known, for example, in Switzerland.

Where to Get Your Unicycle:
You can buy a reasonably priced unicycle in big stores and via the internet, but then you won't get any advice. These cheaper unicycles are often good enough to learn unicycling. However, if you know that you want to do more on a unicycle than just ride it on occasion, it would be a waste of money to buy a reasonably priced one first, only to buy a high quality unicycle shortly thereafter.

We recommend different types of shops mostly for the good advice and service they offer.
There are exceptions to the rule, but the following principles hold true.

Type of Shop:	Advice?	Service?	Recommendation: Buy it here only if you....
Special offers in supermarkets, book stores, ...	No advice	No product selection, no spare parts, no accessories, no (repairing) service	... already know a bit about unicycles, and if you can tell if a unicycle is correctly assembled, and if you can repair it if necessary. ... are looking for a cheaper unicycle.
Internet	No advice	No spare parts, no accessories, no (repairing) service	... already know a bit about unicycles, and if you can tell if a unicycle is correctly assembled, and if you can repair it if necessary. ...are looking for a cheaper unicycle. ...know about the problems of internet trade in general.
Sport specialty shops	Usually you will not get competent advice here because the people in these shops specialize in other sports, and often do not even know that unicycles have a left and right crank	Usually no service, no spare parts, no product selection, but a large assortment of protective gear and accessories	...already know a bit about unicycles, and if you can tell if a unicycle is correctly assembled, and if you can repair it if necessary. ... are looking for a cheaper unicycle. ...can tell the difference between a new unicycle and an old-fashioned one.

Type of Shop:	Advice?	Service?	Recommendation: Buy it here only if you....
Specialty shops for toys	Usually no advice No product selection,	no service, no spare parts, no accessories	...already know a bit about unicycles, and if you can tell if a unicycle is correctly assembled, and if you can repair it if necessary. ...are looking for a cheaper unicycle. ...you can tell the difference between a new unicycle, and an old-fashioned one.
Specialty shops for pedagogical toys	Usually good advice, but often not the latest information on new developments	No selection, no service, no spare parts, few accessories	...already know a bit about unicycles, and if you can tell if a unicycle is correctly assembled, and if you can repair it if necessary. ...are looking for a cheaper unicycle ...can tell the difference between a new unicycle, and an old-fashioned one.
Bicycle shop	Usually the people there try to help you, but often they do not know how to ride a unicycle, and thus, do not know that unicycles have two different cranks	Some repairing service, no spare parts for unicycles available, but they can order most parts, accessories available, protective gear is usually available in BMX specialty shops	...already know a bit about unicycles, and if you can tell if a unicycle is correctly assembled.

Type of Shop:	Advice?	Service?	Recommendation: Buy it here only if you....
Stands at an exhibition or trade fair	Very often most competent person is sitting behind desk, good chance to consult a real expert	Often unicycles are repaired here, or your unicycle can be checked for safety issues, depending on how busy the people are at the fair, many spare parts and accessories available	... want to buy a cheaper old-fashioned unicycle, and get to see the latest unicycles at the same time. ... want to learn more about the latest unicycles, but a large selection is not important to you.
Juggling shops, specialty shops for circus artists,	Good advice given by the person who is responsible for unicycles – usually there is at least one in each shop, Usually there is also one person working in the shop who actually rides unicycles himself; however, he might not be in when you show up Customized unicycles can be ordered, as well Usually the shop also offers wide selection of different brands	Usually good advice is given, good product selection, repairing a unicycle may take several days if the specialist is not in at the moment, all spare parts can be ordered, quite a few spare parts are available in the shop, no protective gear available	... the person who is responsible for unicycles in this shop is selling you the unicycle. ... can see if the unicycle is correctly assembled if this person is not around. ... can avoid high traffic times like Christmas because the people are very busy then, and often do not have time to give you the attention you need.

Type of Shop:	Advice?	Service?	Recommendation: Buy it here only if you....
Specialty shops for unicycles	Great! Tell them exactly what you want, Ask for what they recommend, as well They sell the latest unicycles, and prefer to sell their own brand (often for good reason)	Heaven! Best choice of unicycles and spare parts, all accessories, sometimes they sell only a limited selection of brands	... can arrange it, avoid Christmas time, and any time before a bigger unicycle event or championship. Very often they are very busy at that time, and can not spend as much time on giving advice to you as desirable.

If you know exactly which type of unicycle you want, and if you do not need any advice, you can order your unicycle (even without seeing a picture of it). Nevertheless, it is important to check it out (especially the cranks, etc. ...) as soon as you have received it. If you order it via the internet, it can be very reasonable, but you never know how long this unicycle will really last, and you have no information about the spare parts used. Seat posts can be very short, saddles come without protection, or are made of plastic alone, and the ball bearing might be fixed with a very old-fashioned construction. Every now and then, it happens that the unicycle looks different than the one shown in the picture.

Check it out! Very often instructors or teachers from bigger organizations, or who teach during vacation breaks, have some money left over in the budget to buy unicycles for their organization. They should think carefully if they would not prefer to spend some additional money in order to avoid having to repair the unicycles all the time. Good material pays off quickly, especially when the unicycles are heavily used, as in unicycling courses. It is a good idea to buy unicycles on the internet only if they are really reasonable, and if they do not have to last very long; if they are used in a teaching workshop, they break down very quickly, for example.

127

"The Muni (Mountain Unicycle) or trial unicycle is big, solid and yet not too heavy. Tires, rims, and ball bearings are made extra big, a brake is used to aid your muscles when riding downhill, and thus, some entirely new patterns of movement are possible."

"A size comparison between a 20" and a 24" wheel and a shoe, size 9 1/2"

"14" unicycles are only useful for children who start unicycling at a very young age."

What You Should Know About the Spare Parts of the Unicycle

The Seat Clamp (with Bolt)

There are many different types of seat clamps. Some can be opened and closed very quickly and without extra tools, but they often can not be fixed as tightly as necessary. You should use them if a group of two or three different sized people shares one unicycle, like in a school, a teaching workshop or in a family. Don't mix the spare parts of different seat clamps.

Some cheaper unicycles have seat clamps with a long extended lever which can hurt you. Try to avoid these cheaper variants.

We prefer seat clamps that require an extra tool, like an Allen key® (see next page) as they can be fixed tightly.

An unauthorized, and thus, maybe incompetent adjusting of the saddle is not possible. This is useful if you are the only person to use the unicycle.

These seat clamps are also the best choice in larger groups where more unicycles are in use at the same time, like in a unicycle workshop or at school. The workshop participants should choose a unicycle which has the right size, rather than adjusting the saddle. The teacher holds the only tool which fits to all unicycles if possible. Unicycles are adjusted only if there is no other possibility.

Seat clamps with a thread are sometimes made of aluminum. Do not fix them too tightly for aluminum is softer than steel, and it can easily become deformed.

An Allen key® is not too big, so it is easy to carry it around with you all the time, but you can not fix the clamp as tightly as one with a normal wrench. Therefore, the cheapest construction (with nuts for a normal wrench) is also the tightest one.

If you fix a seat clamp, make sure that the cut in the seat post and the cut in the clamp are in one line, so they can easily close together.

If you have a seat clamp welded to the fork, and you want to exchange it, you can just hit it off carefully with a hammer until it comes loose. This takes only a few hits with a hammer.

Tip:

Make sure that the seat clamp is not fixed too high or too low. It should be 3-4 mm below the end of the fork because the clamp transfers most of its grip at the upper and lower end.

"A good seat clamp is the massive one on the left with an Allen Key®. The clamp on the right can be fixed without an extra tool, but you can not fix it as tightly as necessary. The clamp in the middle is the worst. If you replace its lever with a normal screw, it can be fixed very tightly, and you can not get hurt by the extending lever anymore, but fixing it becomes quite uncomfortable then."

Saddle/Seat

A saddle costs between 5 and 70 $.

Since all people are different, one saddle can be great for one person, and horrible for another. Soft saddles seem to be comfortable at first, but after a short time, the solid metal skeleton inside eventually becomes painful.

Not too long ago, we tested an expensive gel saddle. The idea itself is great, but after a short while it was clear that it caused the same problems as soft saddles.

The Cio saddle is reasonable, and you can take the cover off, and replace the stuffing in the saddle with anything you like. Be careful when you attach the cover again because the laces tend to tear off.

You shouldn't buy a saddle with a plastic skeleton because they break apart in the middle sooner or later. Seams on the cover prove extremely uncomfortable.

Most of the saddles are fixed with four screws to the seat post. If you loosen these screws, you can change the gradient. Try it with the middle position first, and find out how changing the gradient improves your skills. If the saddle pinches you to the front, then make it higher in the front, so that your posture changes when you sit, and you lean back more.

The Shell of the Ball Bearing

This is an important point because cheap unicycles can cause a lot of [trouble].
Closed ball bearing shells made of aluminum (see page 141) might look [a good]
idea, but often they are fixed very poorly to the fork. After a short time [they fall]
apart. There is a very similar construction of high quality by Miyata tho[ugh].
Pichler has created another similar high quality construction where the [inner]
ball bearing is welded to the fork.

The heavier you are, the more money you have to spend on a comfortable saddle (or the less time you can spend on the unicycle).

A handle on the saddle is useful for some tricks, but you do not need it really. If you do tricks where you hold the saddle with one hand, you should check if all screws and sharp edges at the bottom of the saddle are removed or taped.

"Four screws fix the guard to the saddle. The screws which fix the saddle to the seat post can be loosened to adjust the gradient of the saddle."

**"A reasonable and quite solid way to fix the ball bearing to the fo[rk is]
shown here. One shell is welded to the fork, while the other one i[s fixed]
with two screws and nuts."**

A very common and solid way to fix the ball bearing is made of two shells. [Make sure]
that you do not fix the nuts too tightly because the ball bearing might get d[amaged or]
even destroyed otherwise. Although it is made of steel, it is easily affected if [the screws]
are tightened up a bit too much. If the screws of the left on one side are tight[er]
than those on the other side, your unicycle might tend to turn to one side [due to]
the friction. Make sure that the screws are tightened evenly and just as [much as]
necessary to fix the wheel to the fork. The nuts should be on the lower side o[f the fork]
so your trousers do not get caught on them.
    Check the nuts every now and then if they are still properly fixed.

Axle and Hub

These parts have been improved the most over the last few years because there has been great demand for it from the new Trial- and Municyclists. A broken axle causes a lot of trouble because it is expensive and hard to replace.

As soon as a crank is loose even a bit, you should stop riding because your axle gets damaged. Take a break, and fix it properly again. Be careful because often the nut which fixes the crank to the axle can not be tightened as much as needed. The thread at the axle simply "peels off" from many cheaper unicycles, but even with the axle made by Suzue. The longer the lever of your tool is the more carefully it has to be used to tighten the nut.

N&K axles are not very common anymore, but if you have one you can tighten it properly.

Suzue and N&K axles can be easily identified by their labels. They are used in high-quality unicycles like Siegmono or Pichler or sometimes Qu-ax unicycles.
Pichler has recently experimented with an axle of their own production in their latest unicycles. Time will tell how well they work.

Since 2003, splines have been used in Trial- and Mountain unicycle
different cranks have been introduced in order to increase the surf
touching the axle. Thus, they are fixed tighter, and also last longer in
Several manufacturers have started to produce unicycles with di
splines, so there are quite a few different sizes on the market now,
tell yet which one is the best, or will become established as the
Splines are offered with 10-36 cogs.

There are many different hubs, but they all seem to be of the sa
make sure that the hub, rim, and your spokes fit together. The
correct in length and diameter.

The Ball Bearing

All ball bearings are standard industrial size, and you can get ther
shops, but in a specialty shop for unicycles they might be even cheap

For a long time, there was just one size fits all. This made it very ea
ball bearing or the fork. For the new Munis, there is now also anoth
being offered. In order to remove this bearing, you need a professio
can cut it off carefully with a saw or an angle grinder. Be careful no
axle or the hub.

A new bearing has to be fixed with a lot of power. Use a vice if pos
sure that (only) the inside metal ring of the bearing is pushed towar
it slowly forwards. Once it is pushed too far, it is very hard to remove
Normally, ball bearings needn't be replaced. They are closed, and
maintenance although a few drops of oil every now and then may be

---

The Cranks

Depending on the choice of hub, different cranks are required. There are different
variations of splines and other cranks.
Be careful not to ride with loose cranks of any kind because this will invariably
damage the axle, which is hard to repair.

Tip:

If a crank of a unicycle from Taiwan has come loose and can not be fixed any more,
you can try to replace it by a Thun crank, which is a bit smaller and may fit tightly
again.

How do I know how long the cranks should be?

The longer they are, the greater is the leverage, which helps to control the unicycle
on uneven ground. The shorter the cranks are, the faster you can ride and the more
elegant do you look, if you do pirouettes for example. It takes much more force to
accelerate, ride, and slow down a unicycle with short cranks, however.
   For your first unicycle we therefore recommend medium-sized cranks:
   For 16" unicycles, 114mm cranks are medium size are a good medium length.
   For 20" unicycles, 114-127mm are medium size and
   you should choose 125-150mm for 24" unicycles.

The length of the crank is defined as the distance between the center of the hole
where the crank is fixed to the axle and the center of the hole where the pedal is
fixed.

If you want to experiment with different cranks, you need a special tool to remove
them without exercising great force or you ask for help in a bike shop. Put some oil
onto the axle before you remove or fix a new crank. Make sure that you do not mix
up left and right cranks. Right cranks have a normal (clockwise) thread, left cranks
have a left-handed (anti-clockwise) one.

If you replace cranks, your new cranks should only be slightly different to the old
ones because a few millimeters more or less will have a considerable effect.

Cranks are available with the following length: 70, 89, 95, 102, 105, 110, 114, 125,
127, 140, 145, 150, 165 and 170mm. But not all of them are available for all kinds
of axles. Make sure that you have chosen the right length if you want to participate
in an official championship.

The Pedals

You have a huge selection of different pedals since normal bike pedals are compatible with unicycles. A pair of pedals ranges between 5 $ and 90 $. Pedals which are not covered with plastic or rubber, click-pedals, or any construction where the pedal is fixed to the foot are not allowed in official competitions.

Full-metal pedals are also not allowed in some sport halls.

So for a beginner we recommend plastic pedals or rubber pedals, without spikes, because you do not get hurt. Metal pedals with little spikes might be helpful later if your shoes are wet and if you need to keep as much contact to the pedals as possible.

"Cheap plastic pedals are slippery when wet and break easily: if your unicycle topples over, its pedals suffer most in the crash. Good plastic pedals also help to avoid hurting your legs."

Pedals made of one piece of aluminium are very solid but very slippery at the same time, in particular if your shoes are wet. Some pedals offer a bigger platform to stand on and they are less slippery but they are not as solid as normal pedals.

Remember: The left pedal has got a left-handed thread. If you want to fix a new pedal, put some oil on the thread first. Then screw up the first few turns with your hands: right pedal clockwise and left pedal counter-clockwise. With a 15mm wrench you should tighten up the pedal as hard as you can. Don't worry, in this case there is nothing you could damage and only a well-fixed pedal will not come loose again sooner or later while you are riding.

The Spokes

Try to avoid unicycles with plastic spokes and plastic rim. They might look fun but they are not as solid as they should be. If you have a buckled wheel once, you will not be able to repair it because the spokes can not be adjusted. The rim can aslo not be repaired. These unicycles are only useful for very light people.

Although we have never experienced such a case, it might also be dangerous to ride these unicycles because your feet could get stuck between the spokes if you crash in a bad way.

"A unicycle with plastic spokes."

"In a crash the bigger gaps between the spokes could be harmful for your feet."

The cheapest spokes are made of regular steel, with a 2mm diameter. Stainless steel spokes are preferable. They are available for example in 2.3mm or 2.6mm.

It is not always ideal to have your spokes as thick as possible. A 20" unicycle with a total number of 48 extra thick spokes would be so rigid that the spokes would brake more easily than thinner and more flexible ones.

Spokes with 2.6mm and thicker will not fit into all kinds of hubs and rims. Sometimes you can increase the size of the holes in the hub or the rim with a drill but in a rim there are often special eyes which would get destroyed.

Normally unicycles have 28, 36, or 48 spokes. Unicycles with 24 or 32 (for example the triathlon rim) or more than 48 spokes are special constructions.

28 spokes are good enough for kids who are not doing strenuous tricks all the time. 36 spokes are standard. Some manufacturers offer 48-spoke unicycles in their catalogues. If you want more than 48 spokes, you have to do it yourself.

Tip:

Buy a rim and hub manufactured for less spokes, like 28 for example. You can drill an additional hole between each of the existing ones.
If you have got a hub manufactured for 48 spokes, you will not be able to add more holes for additional spokes.

Normally spokes are crossed. Radial spokes are shorter and the peak load for each spoke is higher. 48 spokes in 20" unicycles do not cross or touch each other so they can not get damaged.

36 spokes are good for beginners. You need 36 thicker spokes or 48 normal ones for heavier unicyclists or if you want to do some of the more demanding tricks.

Tip:

A broken spoke should be replaced at once to protect the rim and the other spokes from further damage.

The Seat-post
The saddle is much more important than the seat post. So first try to find a good saddle for you and then get a suitable seat post.

Seat-posts are cheap and easily available in many of the shops mentioned at the end of the book. Normally they can be replaced easily. Just loosen the four nuts (see page 131) and pull off the saddle. Sometimes it can not be removed because it is welded or riveted. Then you have to buy a new saddle if you want a longer post.

Your seat post should be rather too long than too short. You can normally get (spare) seat posts with 20, 30, 40, 50, 60 and 70 cm length. Cutting off a bit is always possible. You just need a metal saw.

Some manufacturers (like Siegmono) offer longer (expensive) seat posts with thicker tubes because long seat posts tend to bend more easily. They are a good, albeit expensive, choice for taller people.

There is a kit available that can be used to prolong Miyata seat-posts as they often turn out to be too short (for Europeans?).

How long should the seat post be depending on body size and wheel size:

body size	wheel size						
	16"	20"	22"	24"	26"	28"	30"
< 120 cm		<20	/	/	/	/	/	/
120-130 cm	20	from 125 cm < 20	/	/	/	/	
130-140 cm	30	20	20	< 20	/	/	/
140-150 cm	30	20	20	20	20	< 20	/
150-160 cm	40	30	30	20	20	20	< 20
160-170 cm	40	30	30	30	20	20	20
170-180 cm	50	40	40	30	30	30	30
180-190 cm	60	50	50	40	30	30	30
190 cm	<70	60	< 60	< 50	40	40	30
length of the seat-post in cm							

This chart is for people with average legs and common unicycle sizes. Sometime also the fork is longer or shorter than usual!

There is a mark a few inch before the end. This shows you the minimum length of the seat-post that should stay in the fork. If this mark is missing, you should draw it at least 8cm before the end.

BMX seat posts are very durable but they can only be fixed to a limited number of saddles.

Seat posts are made of steel or aluminium. There is only one standard size for unicycles (22mm diamter) and another one for Trial and Mountain unicycles (25.4mm). Most of them are chromium-plated, others are black or red.

Seat posts with a smooth surface tend to twist more easily. You can use sandpaper or some sand to make the surface rough. Do NOT put oil on your seat post.

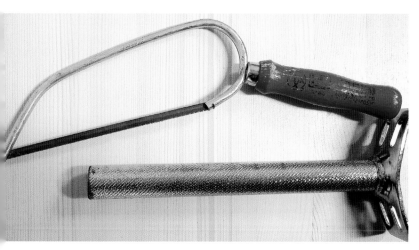

"Don't be afraid of cutting off the seat post yourself if the saddle is too high for you in the lowest position. A spare seat post is cheap and easily available."

The Profile and tyre
Your single wheel carries a lot of weight. Make sure that you have enough air pressure. New tyres can be inflated with a little bit more pressure than recommended on the tyre. For cross-country riding and with older tyres you should stay a bit below the recommended pressure. If you haven't got enough pressure, your unicycle will drift to the side, keeping the balance gets more difficult, and tyre, tube, and rim may get damaged.

There is a huge selection of tyres in different sizes, traeds and colors so we can only roughly outline the most basic formats. If you buy a new tyre you have to check if it is as broad and as big as your rim.

The most common size is 20"x1.75" (1"=2.54cm). The first number refers to the diameter, the second refers to how broad your tyre is. Normally 1.75" tyres can also be replaced with 1.95" tyres. Tyres of 2" breadth or more may not fit between the posts of your fork.

If you ride indoors, you should check if all tyres or only light-coloured ones are permitted. Normally, all tyres that are not black are considered light-coloured even if red tyres for example leave just as bad marks on the floor as black ones. By the way, it depends more on the floor than on the tyre if rubber comes of the tryes. A tyre leaves rub-marks on one floor but not on another one.

Black tyres are normally of a higher quality. On asphalt your tyres wear off more easily, so black ones are useful here. Even if a black tyre is totally worn off and looks like a slick, it will still keep better contact to the floor than a light-coloured tyre with a new tread.

According to rumors some new light-coloured tyres are supposed to be better than black ones but we haven't seen any of them yet.

Bright tyres are very good for ultimates because they do not keep good contact to your legs!

Try to test different types of tyres. There are Slicks for indoor use, Cross for outdoor and Negative Profile and normal Profile for all-round use. The most expensive tyre is not necessarily the best one for you.

Smooth tyres with high air pressure, like the Panaracer, are very suitable for pirouettes. The Generixx and Maxxis are high-pressure tyres as well. They can be used well on smooth surfaces but the delicate profile is quickly worn off.

Since 20" is a common BMX size as well, there is the biggest range of colors and qualities available here, compared to a very limited range for 16" and 22". 24" is a common size again for children's bikes and for wheelchairs as well. Consequently, there is a wide range of light colors (e.g. for wheelchairs) and different qualities.

"This is an ideal tyre for indoor use: light-coloured and with little tread."

"Other colors are available for indoor use, at least for 20" wheels."

"Ball bearings in aluminium shells fixed to a simple metal tube of the fork are a nuisance because they break apart sooner or later."

The Fork

The frame of a unicycle consists only of the fork. The shells for the ball bearing can be seen as part of this frame. Some manufacturers offer extra long forks for extra big people for extra money.

There is a wide range of forks, chromium-plated and colored, in one or more colors, with square tubes or round ones and with bent or welded tubes (see photos p. 128 and 140), with extra wide seat post tubes, with fixed seat clamp or with hooks for the brakes.

The way in which the ball-bearing is fixed to the fork is most important. As you can see on the photo above, some shells holding the ball bearings are fixed to the fork with two horizontal screws. This is a cheap but unsatisfactory solution because the metal of the fork is normally too soft to withstand the forces at work here and sooner or later the fork breaks apart (see photo). If you find such a construction, do NOT buy the unicycle.

Buying a fork from a different brand than the rest of your unicycle can prove problematic as it usually is not compatible.

If you buy a fork of the same brand, you should take care about the following things:
• chromium-plated forks are more resistant to scratches; colored forks look nicer (and usually ecologically less harmfully manufactured)

- many tricks are more easy with a fork with a square instead of a round connection between the upper tube and the two lower tubes (see photo). The latter is only useful for people with stronger legs for they might get hurt at the edges.
- make sure that the ball bearings are as far apart as the fork
- make sure that the ball bearings fit into the fork. There can be problems with the new Munis

The tube which holds the seat-post should be smooth on the inside. There shouldn't be any grates left from cutting or welding. Sometimes the seat post can not be pushed (completely) into the tube because of bad craftsmanship here. The tube for the seat-post should be quite short (about 15 cm) if the unicycle is to be used by children because the lowest possible position of the saddle is otherwise still too high.

"This kind of construction is very useful for many tricks as it offers a good place to your foot or to stand on e.g. when you ride with one leg or with two people on one unicycle."

The Rim
The price for a rim can vary considerably. The more money you spend here, the better is the quality you will get in general. However, a simple steel rim is more resistant to scratches and bumps and it is fine for simple riding and for your first tricks but you shouldn't jump or ride down bigger steps with it. Personally, I prefer steel rims for races because they have more momentum and they run quite smoothly because they are heavier. If you want to do jumps, we recommend rims made of aluminium. Make sure that the number of eyes for the spokes in the rim matches those of your hub.

"Rims of aluminium are also available in nice colors."

The Wheel

The wheel consists of the following components: tyre, rim, rim tape, tube and valve, hub, axle and ball bearings (!). If you order a complete wheel, make sure that you mention all components you want or do not want to avoid misunderstandings. Tell them also if you want cranks and pedals as well.

Tips on maintenance and repairing unicycles:

Important:

Many unicycles get damaged because they have been assembled in the wrong way around, i.e. by mixing up left and right cranks and pedals. Unfortunately this may even happen if it was assembled by a "specialist shop."
Check your new unicycle. It is worth the effort!

You can tell whether your unicycle has been correctly assembled if the left pedal is in fact on the left side and the right pedal is at the right side. If they are not in the correct place, it is very likely that the pedals are screwed off sooner or later by the constant turn of the pedals when riding. The worst case is that you suddenly loose your pedal while you are riding and I can tell you (from experience?) that is one thing you surely do not want to happen!

Your unicycle also might get badly damaged long before your pedal actually comes off.

This is how a unicycle is assembled correctly and how you can check whether it has be done properly:

First check which is the right and which the left cranks and whether the correct pedal is in the crank. The wrong pedal might have been forcefully screwed into the wrong crank. Unfortunately this might look ok at first glance and even hold fast for a while until it suddenly comes off. If the unicycle has been assembled in the wrong way, the thread of the pedals and cranks are destroyed and the pedals can not be exchanged later on.

On each crank on the inside, there is a "R" or "L" which refers to "right" and "left" of course. You will find the same capital letters on the pedals.

"The capital letters "R" and L" can be found on each crank and on each pedal. Make sure that they match."

So first you assemble the cranks and the pedals correctly (or check them). After having assembled the cranks and pedals correctly (or having checked that this has been done properly), you fix the cranks to the axle of the wheel. It **doesn't** matter which crank you fix to which side of the wheel but it is important that the wheel with the cranks is fixed correctly to the fork.

The fork has got a **cut** of 3-5 cm at the **back** of the tube where the seat-post goes in (see photo). This cut helps that the seat clamp can squeeze the tube more effectively to hold the seat-post properly. When you fix the saddle to the fork, make sure that the broad back part of the saddle shows to the back where this cut is in the fork.

"The broad end of the saddle is the back side. It should be at the same side as the cut in the fork. The seat clamp should also be open at the side of the cut!"

Because the saddle has a clearly defined back and front, it follows logically at which side the left and the right crank have to be if you refer to the saddle. Saddle, seat clamp, cut in the fork, and cranks and pedals have to be correctly assembled.

The right crank has got a normal thread but the left crank has got a left-handed thread.

If you thus ride forwards with a correctly assembled unicycle, each turn of the wheel and therefore of the pedals helps to tighten the pedals on the cranks. But if your saddle points to the wrong direction in relationship to your cranks and pedals, as it might happen after fixing the cranks to the wrong side or, more often, after adjusting the height of the saddle (!!), the pedals will loosen with each turn of your cycle. This will even happen if the pedals were fixed tightly because the pedals often get loose by frequent crashes of the unicycle. Remember that the unicycle mostly crashes on the pedals!

Therefore you should be careful when you adjust the height of your saddle. Check from time to time if all screws are still tight. You can do this simply by listening to the noise your unicycle makes. A unicycle is built quite compact. If you hear a rattling noise after the unicycle has crashed to the floor, you can be sure that at least one screw has to be tightened. For this reason you shouldn't fix anything (like bells, toys or beads) to your unicycle which might rattle all the time and thus cover the noise of loose parts of your unicycle.

Any loose screws can destroy the thread if it is not tightened again soon. Pedals can be pulled very tight indeed. Buying the proper tool to fix them pays off quickly in larger groups like schools where many unicycles are in use.

For the reasons given above, the saddles should only be adjusted by people who know how to handle them properly. If you teach beginners classes, make sure that nobody manipulates the saddles without being supervised. Even if the saddle is not adjusted in height but only wrenched to the side, beginners tend to twist it around to the wrong side every now and then, in particular if one unicycle is shared by different riders. Therefore we recommend seat clamps with an AllenKey® kept in safe custody by the instructor (and by a few other well-informed people).

A quick way to adjust saddles which have been wrenched to the side:
you should try if you can adjust the saddle again without opening the seat clamp. Sometimes the seat clamp is fixed very tightly but the saddle can be twisted quite easily nevertheless because the seat clamp is damaged or not adjusted properly. After you have tried to adjust the saddle, you can tighten the seat clamp a bit more as well.

Normally the saddle is solid enough to be adjusted without opening the seat clamp. Put one leg over the unicycle and hold the saddle with both hands at the front and the back. Block the wheel with your legs and adjust the saddle by gaining momentum only from your hip.

However, if you wrench the saddle to adjust it without loosening the seat clamp, you might damage the seat-post in the long run and it might get twisted even faster after some time. This can be a problem if it is not your own unicycle. On the other hand, a new seat-post is not very expensive. So you have to decide whether you want to adjust the saddle the quick way or not.

Tips on how to store a large number of unicycles:

Unicycles can be hanged from the ceiling in a line with hooks. With a long chain you can link them together and lock them if the storage room is used by other groups as well.

**"Use your hip to gain momentum.
The saddle and the wheel are just held
by hands and legs."**

There is another thread at the axle where the crank is fixed with a nut. If this thread is damaged, then the whole unicycle is out of order and it is very expensive and difficult to repair this thread because it is directly cut into the axle.

How to protect your unicycle:

When you practice unicycling, the pedals and the saddle get damaged most. If you want to protect your unicycle, you can try to catch the saddle before it crashes to the floor. Catch it from behind you when you have to dismount. But make sure that you protect yourself first! Not getting hurt yourself should be your top priority. It is nice if you can take care of your unicycle as well without neglecting yourself and you should practice it. Beginners are often very concerned about their unicycle but when they try to protect their unicycle from any damage, they block their natural reactions and reflexes which help to ride the unicycle. So in fact they obstruct their learning progress and do not learn how to ride the unicycle properly.

Remember: the unicycle is designed to "survive" quite a number of crashes and it is more durable than you might think!

b)   The Giraffe

The most common wheel size of giraffes are 20" and 24". If you want to use a bigger wheel, check whether the fork is big enough for it.

A giraffe with a 20" wheel looks more impressive, but 24" is easier to ride on uneven surfaces.

Remember: It is just as easy to ride a giraffe as a normal unicycle. It is just more exhilarating.

There are giraffes with two double poles and giraffes with one pole only. Some giraffes can be adjusted in height with tubes of different length, like the Pichler Flex. Others can be folded or taken apart, like the Pichler Travel.

There are quite cheap giraffes from Asia which are still good enough for normal use and more expensive high quality giraffes made in Europe.

If you want to do shows, you should definitely spend some extra money for a better quality.

Normally one chain is sufficient but you can also buy a giraffe with two chains or with a drive belt.

Do not grease your chain too often because you can not avoid touching it from time to time.

There are also variations of giraffes with more than one wheel (called Twice, Trice, and Manywheel). The momentum is transferred from the upper wheel to the lower one. Many other special constructions are possible as well.

If you have a giraffe with a chain, you can also, for example, get gears for your giraffe. Be careful because riding a giraffe even with a moderate gear ratio is harder than you might think.

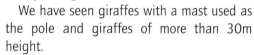

We have seen giraffes with a mast used as the pole and giraffes of more than 30m height.

Always remember: stow away your shoelaces properly so that they do not get caught in the chain or the pedal. This would be disastrous.

You can also get hurt badly if your fingers get drawn between chain and cogwheel.

"This chain is not tight enough. The movement of your feet is not transmitted properly to the wheel."

"The left big nut is used to fix the position of the chain, the smaller nut on the right is used to tighten the chain."

The correct tension of the chain helps to properly transmit the movement of the feet to the wheel. If the chain is too slack, the movement of your feet is transferred to the wheel with delay. Tighten up your chain before you get into trouble. If the tension is too high though it will slow down your movements or even get ripped apart. If you want to tighten or loose the chain, first loosen the big nut, which fixes the position of the chain, then loosen the smaller nut.

Clothing

You do not need special clothing to ride a unicycle. Nevertheless a few things may be important to know:

Sturdy shoes with a good tread and without heels are useful. Some artists prefer very soft shoes because they help to feel the pedals better but they protect your feet less. Shoes like chucks protect your ankles but often the soles of these shoes are a bit slippery. Chucks with soft spikes of bright rubber would be perfect but we haven't seen anything like that yet. You can also get an extra protection for your ankles as used by people who play soccer.

Do not practice any tricks on the unicycle without wearing shoes.

Remember:

The shoe laces should be kept short so they can not get caught in the pedals or the chain.

Your trousers shouldn't be too long or wide so they do not get caught by the cranks or pedals. A good choice are cycling shorts with inset. Especially for males they increase comfort a lot!

Cycling gloves and protectors for your knees may help as well but they are not necessary. Sometimes they even obstruct your movements. Some people wear helmets and some protection for their teeth, especially when they are playing unicyclehockey.

For advanced trial-cycling gloves, helmets, and knee protection are compulsory. In races knee protection and gloves are compulsory as well.

Do not wear protectors designed for volleyball because they can not be fixed as tightly as necessary. Try the more solid knee protectors used by skaters. I wear them in unicyclehockey matches as well. In advanced trial-unicycling you should wear protectors for your shins, and wrists as well. Make sure that your protectors are "air-conditioned." You do not have to spend a lot of money on protectors as sometimes the cheap protectors are quite good. Make sure you are protected everywhere you need it, including the lower part of your leg.

Try to avoid (costumes with) long dresses, skirts or long coats for they can be caught in the wheel as well.

c)   The Ultimate

The best size by far is 24". The pedals should not extend to far from the wheel to make it run evenly. Do rather buy a real ultimate than taking off the fork from your unicylce as a real ultimate is much better and easier to ride.

The more distance there is between the two pedals and the closer they are thus to the rim, the more easy the ultimate is to pedal it forward but the more difficult it gets to keep the balance. Nevertheless, the optimal distance from one pedal to the other is quite short, about 24-25 cm for a 24" ultimate.

The tyre should have no profile at all if possible. The best tyre you can get is an old, worn off tyre from a 24" unicycle or wheelchair. Keep it somewhere outdoors for a whole winter so that the rubber looses its grip and runs better along your legs. If you have to buy a new wheel, buy one designed for wheelchairs (you can get them in a special shop for orthopaedic aids). These tyres often have only a low profile and no profile at the sides. They are light-coloured and can be used indoors everywhere.

High boots or chaps used in horse riding can be quite useful as well. They are made of leather and they cover the lower leg and your knee. If they are thoroughly greased they run along your ultimate very smoothly. It is a great feeling. Unfortunately the grease usually dries up in a few minutes and then the riding gets much more difficult than without chaps and. So they are only useful if you want to perform a short act.

An alternative to leather is neoprene. Buy the light neoprene knee protectors used for volleyball matches (see photo). Wear them a bit lower than usual over your jeans.

"Good protectors made of neoprene are very useful on the ultimate."

You can also try to cover your tyre somehow along the sides. Silicon spray is recommended by many people. Other possibilities are to paint or lacquer it or to cover it with gaffertape to reduce the friction against your legs. Most of these solutions do not last very long so my advice is to simply learn the proper riding technique as well. An ultimate can be ridden without even touching the tyre at all! This makes you entirely independent from any additional material. Good material is just useful if you want to learn a new trick or do a performance. However, if you practice a new and difficult trick or want to be on the safe side during a performance, you can well use the protective equipment.

2 Some Useful Websites:

http://www.unicycling.org/usa

http://unicycling.org

http://www.unicycle.org.uk
union of UK unicyclists

http://www.tcuc.org
Twin Cities Unicycle Club in Minnesota / USA

http://www.unicycling.org/iuf
International Unicycling Federation

http://www.unicycling.org/iuf/rulebook

http://unicyclist.org

http://www.unicycle.net
fun stuff

http://www.schulseiten.de/kjw/einrad.html
German site

http://www.ibrmv.de/html/body_einrad.htm
lGerman site

http://www.unicykel.com
Danish site

http://www.gilby.com

http://www.japan-
net.ne.jp/~mhayashi/ichirin
Japanese site

http://unicycle.eyume.com
Singapore site

http://monocycle.info
French site

http://www14.plala.or.jp/uni-
nagisa/nagisa/index.html
Japanese site with many links

http://www.unicycling.org.au
Australian Unicycle Society, official website

http://www.unicyclingnt.com
Unicycling Association of the Northern
Territory (Australia)

http://rsc.anu.edu.au/~pdc/acturs
Australian site, Canberra

http://www.unicycling.net/canadian.htm
Canadian site

http://www.unicycle.or.kr/index.htm
Korean site

http://www.unicycle.or.kr/english/index_
english.htm
Korean site in English

http://www.uniciclismo.com
basketball on unicycles, Puerto Rico

3   Some Retailers:

http://www.koxx-one.com

www.bedfordunicycles.ca

www.krisholm.com

http://www.ajata.de/ratshop

http://www.municycle.com
international shop

http://einradshop.ch
Swiss shop

http://www.pichlerrad.de
German shop

http://siegmono.de
German shop

http://unicycle.com
American shop

http://unicycle.uk.com
European shop

Thanks

to Dr. Mark Berninger for his help with the translation

Photo and Illustration Credits

Cover design:	Sabina Groten
Cover photos:	Andreas Anders-Wilkens
	© [Dynamic Graphics]/[liquidlibrary]/Thinkstock
Inside Photos:	Oskar Bauer, Robert Mager, Andreas Anders-Wilkens